HER DARLING BOY

HER DARLING BOY

The letters of a mother, her beloved son,
and the heartbreaking cost of Vimy Ridge

Tom Goodman

GREAT PLAINS
PUBLICATIONS

Great Plains Publications
233 Garfield Street
Winnipeg, MB R3G 2M1
www.greatplains.mb.ca

Great Plains Publications gratefully acknowledges the financial support provided for its publishing program by the Government of Canada through the Canada Book Fund; the Canada Council for the Arts; the Province of Manitoba through the Book Publishing Tax Credit and the Book Publisher Marketing Assistance Program; and the Manitoba Arts Council.

Design & Typography by Relish New Brand Experience
Printed in Canada by Friesens

LIBRARY AND ARCHIVES CANADA CATALOGUING IN PUBLICATION

Goodman, Tom, author
    Her darling boy : a tale of Vimy Ridge / Tom Goodman.

Includes index.
Issued in print and electronic formats.
ISBN 978-1-927855-47-8 (paperback).--ISBN 978-1-927855-52-2 (epub).--
ISBN 978-1-927855-53-9 (mobi)

    1. Goodman, Tom--Family. 2. Vimy Ridge, Battle of, France, 1917.
3. World War, 1914-1918--France. 4. World War, 1914-1918--Canada.
I. Title.

D545.V5G65 2016   940.4'31   C2016-902043-6
                                       C2016-902044-4

ENVIRONMENTAL BENEFITS STATEMENT

Great Plains Publications saved the following resources by printing the pages of this book on chlorine free paper made with 100% post-consumer waste.

TREES	WATER	ENERGY	SOLID WASTE	GREENHOUSE GASES
12	5,834	6	390	1,076
FULLY GROWN	GALLONS	MILLION BTUs	POUNDS	POUNDS

Environmental impact estimates were made using the Environmental Paper Network Paper Calculator 3.2. For more information visit www.papercalculator.org.

Canadä

FSC
www.fsc.org
MIX
Paper from
responsible sources
FSC™ C016245

Dedicated to the memory of Pte. Archibald John Polson a soldier of
The Great War and Elísabet Thuríður Polson his loving mother.

CONTENTS

THE MYTH OF VIMY

IN 1798, ENGLISH POET LAUREATE ROBERT SOUTHEY wrote an anti-war poem called *The Battle of Blenheim*. He tells of a young boy named Peterkin who comes to his grandfather, Kaspar, with a skull he has found while playing in a nearby battlefield. The old man says it is the skull of a fallen soldier, and that he often finds such skulls while tilling his garden. He goes on to tell the boy in chilling detail of the battle's carnage, and says such things must be in a famous victory. At the end of the poem, Peterkin asks his grandfather a final question:

> "But what good came of it at last?"
> Quoth little Peterkin.
> "Why, that I cannot tell," said he,
> "But 'twas a famous victory."

In April of 1917, my uncle, Private Archibald John Polson, was a machine gunner stationed at the foot of Vimy Ridge, the site of the Canadian army's most famous victory of World War 1. Like Robert Southey's battle, the bloody victory at Vimy Ridge has been celebrated by the generations that followed. And, also like Southey's battle, Vimy was a mythic event whose myth has obscured what really happened.

When I was a boy, Uncle Archie was little more to me than a handsome young man in uniform pictured in a framed photograph that hung on our wall. That all changed a few years ago when I came across a treasure trove of Archie's wartime correspondence with my grandmother. The photo on the wall suddenly came to life as a remarkable family story unfolded. It is my privilege, perhaps my duty, to tell you that story.

Military history as recounted by professional historians can be a dry read, filled with facts about strategy and execution, victories and defeats, but with little sense of the real life experience of the ordinary soldiers who fight and die. Also, the interpretation of military history is often skewed by the rhetoric of generals and politicians, who, like old Kaspar, tend to revel in victory, exaggerating its significance and discounting its cost. They are also inclined to claim noble purpose for their actions.

Regarding the latter point, consider World War 1, referred to at the time as The Great War. There have been many generals and politicians who would have you believe that World War 1 was undertaken by the British and their allies in the defence of freedom, or for some other great and noble purpose.[1] In reality, there was nothing great or noble about The Great War. Rather, it was the unintended consequence of ill-considered foreign policies conducted by the nations of Europe in the early 1900s.

In those days, Europe was a patchwork of adversarial alliances. When Archduke Ferdinand of Austria and his wife were assassinated in June of 1914, there was a ripple effect, pitting alliance against alliance. Provocative acts escalated into acts of aggression and, within a few months, war was declared by most European nations, including by Great Britain against Germany and Austria-Hungary.

It was a total failure of international diplomacy, or as the British wartime prime minister, David Lloyd George, put it in his memoirs:

> How was it that the world was so unexpectedly plunged into this terrible conflict? Who was responsible? Not even the astutest [sic] and most far-seeing statesman foresaw in the early summer of 1914 that the autumn would find the nations of the world interlocked in the most terrible conflict that had ever been witnessed in the history of mankind. [...] The nations slithered over the brink into the boiling cauldron of war.[2]

As I have mentioned, I am going to tell you the story of my Uncle Archie, an ordinary Canadian soldier of that "most terrible conflict", but first of all, I must tell you about the Battle of Vimy Ridge, because Vimy was when everything changed for Archie and his family.

Until I started to research this book, I had understood that, despite its terrible cost, the victory at Vimy Ridge was a proud moment for Canadians because:

a. Vimy marked a profound turning-point in the War,[3] and
b. it was the first occasion on which all four divisions of the Canadian Corps fought as one unit, and thus marked the birth of our nation.[4]

The attack on Vimy Ridge took place in 1917, three years after the outbreak of the war. As a British colony, Canada had automatically become a combatant when Great Britain declared war, and the Canadian Corps fought as a contingent of the British Expeditionary Force. Things were not going well for the Canadians by 1917. Casualties were heavy and the government was considering the imposition of conscription, an unpopular measure in the province of Quebec and among farmers.

World War I was fought largely along a battle line across France that was known as The Western Front. In April of 1917, the Canadian Corps occupied trenches adjacent to Vimy Ridge, a strategically important point along The Western Front. The French planned a major offensive, later known as the Nivelle Offensive, and the British undertook the Battle of Arras in support. The battle officially commenced on April 9, 1917 when the British advanced against the Germans at Arras, and the Canadians captured nearby Vimy Ridge. Australian and additional British troops joined the fray at Bullecourt on April 11th, and the battle continued until the middle of May.

The attack on Vimy Ridge has become known in Canada as The Battle of Vimy Ridge, but it was not categorized as a battle at the time, and no military historian outside Canada considers Vimy to be more than just one part of the Battle of Arras.[5]

So, was Vimy a great victory that marked a turning point in the war? Canadian historian J.L. Granatstein rebutted this assertion in his book, *The Greatest Victory: Canada's One Hundred Days, 1918*. In arguing that the Canadian victories from August to November of 1918 were of far greater significance, he has acknowledged that Vimy was a great morale boost but wrote:

> Vimy was part of a major British offensive on the Arras front, and the British Expeditionary Force, commanded by Field Marshall Sir Douglas Haig, made some small gains. The taking of Vimy Ridge in a carefully planned set piece was the highlight of the offensive, to be sure, but Haig and his commanders had no plans for exploitation, and there was no massed cavalry division waiting in the rear ready to fan out over German-occupied territory to turn the enemy's tactical defeat into a strategic rout. All that happened, important as it was, was that the Germans retreated a few miles eastward into new trench lines in front of the industrial and mining town of Lens, where the Canadians would fight into the summer of 1917. Vimy unfortunately did not change the war or even substantially change its course.[6]

Sir John Keegan, probably the greatest military historian of the 20th century, went even further in his book entitled *The First World War*. While he praised the Canadian troops, he wrote that our success was only achieved because of a pair of German blunders:

> [The Germans'] setback at Vimy had had two causes: first, an expectation that the British bombardment would last longer than it did, and a consequent failure to bring their counter-attack provisions forward in sufficient time to intervene, but second, an absolute deficiency in divisions on the Arras-Vimy sector.[7]

Finally, what about the claim that the attack marked the birth of Canada as a nation? This proposition was first advanced by Brigadier General Alexander Ross, the commander of the 28th (North–West) Battalion at Vimy, who wrote:

> From dugouts, shell holes and trenches, men sprang into action, fell into military formations and advanced to the ridge—every division of the corps moved forward together. It was Canada from the Atlantic to the Pacific on parade. I thought then, and I think today, that in those few minutes, I witnessed the birth of a nation.[8]

Ross's grand declaration has been challenged by credible academics. Major John R. Grodzinski, CD, Ph.D., a career military officer and an assistant professor at the Royal Military College, published an article on Vimy in the *Canadian Military Journal* in 2009.

> [The victory at Vimy Ridge] did not establish Canadian nationhood—that came through a sense of confidence developed during the entirety of the war itself, where a self-governing colony gave much of itself to a cause, and, in the process, changed. The notion of soldiers coming down Vimy Ridge as Canadians was not expressed in 1917, but it was fabricated by a series of leading questions directed to Great War veterans during the 1960s.[9]

Jean Martin, a historian with the Directorate of History and Heritage at Canadian National Defence Headquarters, has been even more blunt in his criticism. In 2011, Martin also published an article on the subject in the *Canadian Military Journal*. He wrote:

> The battle of Vimy Ridge has nothing to do with the birth of the Canadian nation. A reasonable case could be made that it was an important event in Canada's history, but to claim that the nation was born on 9 April 1917, on the Artois plains is to deny more than three centuries of history during which the ancestors of millions of Canadians devoted their lives to building this country. If Canada was born in the trenches of France and Belgium between 1915 and 1918, it was only in the minds of a few thousand soldiers who had very shallow roots there. In the minds of most of its inhabitants, Canada had already existed for a long time.[10]

At the end of the day, there is but one important truth about our "famous victory" at Vimy Ridge: it resulted in the death or injury, often horrible injury, of more than 10,000 Canadian soldiers—including "the single bloodiest day in Canadian military history", according to our present Governor-General[11]—as well as the death or injury of 20,000 Germans.[12] Canadian losses were so significant that the Canadian government was forced to invoke conscription in order to raise more troops, a measure that deeply divided our nation.[13]

Perhaps, the most succinct assessment of Vimy was given by the late Mrs. Charlotte Susan Wood, Canada's first Silver Cross mother, when she was introduced to King Edward VIII at the unveiling of the Vimy Memorial in France in 1935.

"Oh, Sir," she said, "I have just been looking at the trenches and I just can't figure out why our boys had to go through that."[14]

What follows is the story of one immigrant family, and how Vimy Ridge forever altered their lives—in particular, the life of one of those "boys" to whom Mrs. Wood referred, and the life of his mother. Archie Polson's story is revealed in extensive wartime correspondence maintained by the family and in the Archie Polson fonds at the University of Manitoba Archives, and has now been fully transcribed, annotated and, in the case of many of the letters, translated from Icelandic.

Archie Polson was born on November 25, 1895, and grew up in Gimli, Manitoba. He enlisted as a private in the Canadian army in February of 1916, and trained at Camp Hughes, near Carberry, Manitoba. Archie went overseas in September, 1916, with the 2nd Divisional Machine Gun Corps, first to Witley Military Camp, located about forty miles south of London, and then to the Canadian Military Depot in Crowborough, Sussex where he took machine gun training. He was posted to France early in February, 1917, and was at the Front by month's end.

The attack on Vimy Ridge is commemorated on April 9 each year, but the action took much longer than one day. The first phase commenced on April 2, 1917, when the Canadian artillery attacked the enemy's trenches with a withering barrage that lasted for a week. The actual charge took place on Easter Monday, April 9, with the control of the ridge achieved late on April 12. Archie was seriously wounded on April 5 when an enemy shell exploded near him.

Archie spent many months recovering in military hospitals in England, most of that time in Stockport, near Manchester, and later in Ramsgate, on the Strait of Dover, when he was ready to return home.

Throughout his time in the service, Archie maintained an active correspondence, mostly with his mother, Elísabet, but also with his father, his siblings, his friends and his comrades. Elísabet retained many of the letters that she received from Archie, as well as official communications from government officials and correspondence from various Canadian Red Cross officials updating the family on the progress of Archie's recovery. Archie likewise kept most of the letters that he received. Taken together, the letters, both personal and bureaucratic, provide an insight into the young soldier's experience during the War, and the life of his family back at home.

CHAPTER ONE

IN THE BEGINNING

TO PROPERLY UNDERSTAND ARCHIE POLSON, it is important to know something about the immigrant culture in which he lived, and how his family found their way to Manitoba in the first place.

Archie's parents, Ágúst (pronounced *Ow-goost*) and Elísabet (pronounced *El-ees-a-bet*), were two of the many thousands of desperate Icelanders who immigrated to Canada between 1870 and 1915. This was a difficult period in Icelandic history. First, there was a series of widespread crop failures, and small expeditions began to leave the country. Then, in 1875, Mount Askja erupted, depositing a thick layer of acidic ash on settlements across many parts of Iceland, poisoning the land and killing the livestock. The Icelandic economy was devastated, and there was widespread famine. With that, the trickle of emigrants turned into a torrent.

Ultimately, a quarter of the nation's population settled in Canada. The Liberal government of the day had a policy of encouraging immigration to the western provinces, and Manitoba was the destination of choice for the great majority of Icelanders. Even now, so many years after the first migration, there are almost 89,000 citizens of Icelandic origin living in Canada (according to the 2006 Canadian census) compared to the total population of Iceland of 330,000.

The Governor-General of Canada, Lord Dufferin, assisted the Icelanders in the establishment of a semi-autonomous Icelandic reserve called "New Iceland", about 58 kilometers north to south along the west side of Lake Winnipeg, plus Hecla Island. This area was chosen so that the Icelanders could farm and fish, two of their traditional occupations, but many of them would later end up in Winnipeg.

Archie Polson's mother came to Canada in 1876 with the first large group. She was seven years old. Her full name was Elísabet Thuriður Gísladóttir, her surname based on the Icelandic patronymic practice.

Under this system, a person's surname is his or her father's first name plus "son" or "dóttir", as the case may be. In Iceland, the emphasis is on a person's first name, so, for example, to this day alphabetical listings in Icelandic phone books are based on first names. An Icelandic woman does not change her surname when she marries.

The Icelanders abandoned the patronymic system after they arrived in Canada, and many shortened or anglicized their surnames in order to make them less challenging for English speakers. In addition, the practice of women's surnames including the suffix "dóttir" also died out and the Icelandic women started to take their husbands' surnames upon marriage.

The reader should also be aware that pronunciation of Icelandic names can be tricky for English speakers. Without getting too technical, you should know that 'ð' is pronounced as a soft *th* and the letter 'J' or 'j' is silent. An acute accent above a vowel means it is a short vowel, but pronounced differently than an English short vowel. So, while Jón is pronounced *Yoan*, 'Á' or 'á' is pronounced *ow*, 'É' or 'é' is pronounced is *ay*, 'Í' or 'í' is pronounced *ee* and 'Ú' or 'ú' is pronounced *oo*.

In the early 1860s, Elísabet's mother, Thuriður Elísabet Jónsdóttir,[15] and her husband, Árni, lived on a farm known as *Marbæli* in the Skagafjörður district of northern Iceland. They had four children, born between 1860 and 1866. In 1864, Thuriður and Árni moved to another farm in the same district, *Krithóll*, but the move proved to be a bad omen, because Árni died shortly afterwards, at the age of 32. After Árni's death, Thuriður realized that she could not operate the farm by herself, especially given that she had four young children to support. So she hired a young man, Gísli Konráð Eiriksson, to help her.

Despite a twelve-year age gap, Thuriður and Gísli became romantically involved, and after a time, lived as man and wife. They must have seemed a rather unlikely couple, and not just because of the difference in their ages. Thuriður was tough, resilient and dominant. Gísli, on the other hand, had more refined tastes, having been born into a family of brilliant writers and thinkers.[16] Thuriður was deeply in love with her young partner, while Gísli's affection seems to have been founded, at least to some extent, on proximity and opportunity.

In those days, itinerant ministers travelled from the Icelandic capital of Reykjavík to remote rural communities just once a year. Because the banns had to be read aloud three times during consecutive church services prior to marriage, and services were held so infrequently, getting married could take a long time. Many couples lived together for an extended period before they were married, and often already had children together.

Thuriður and Gísli had two children, Elísabet, who was born in 1869, and a younger brother, Konráð, who died in infancy. Thuriður was 39 years of age when her daughter, Elísabet, was born, and Gísli was 27.

Given the differences in their ages and in their temperaments, it is not surprising that there were strains in their relationship. As well, these were stressful times for many people in Iceland. Icelandic-Canadian genealogist and historian, Nelson Gerrard in his book, *Icelandic River Saga: A History of the Icelandic River and Ísafold Settlements*, describes the situation this way:

> Nineteenth-century Iceland was [...] a bleak and forbidding land shrouded by hardship and suffering—a place of gnawing hunger, bitter cold, grim pestilence, and baleful oppression. These were largely the result of a harsh environment, characterized by intermittent sieges of polar ice and fiery volcanic eruptions—but there were deeply rooted social and economic problems as well, including overpopulation, disparity, underdevelopment and trade monopolization—all of which led to a general state of disillusionment and misery for large segments of the population. Those who left Iceland during these years did so for a multitude of reasons—personal, economic, social, political and religious—all of them considerations most of us can scarcely understand a hundred or more years later in our land of plenty and our society of personal freedom above all else.[17]

Sometime after the banns had been read for the second time, but before their marriage was solemnized, Gísli abandoned his family. To make matters worse for Thuriður and her children, the calamitous eruption of Mount Askja occurred in 1875, resulting in the destruction of Thuriður's farm. So a year later, Thuriður, now 46 and with little to lose, packed up her five children and joined a group of 1,200 emigrants bound for Manitoba. Like many of the indigent people in the group, her fare and that of her children was likely paid by the local government where they resided in order to get them off the welfare rolls.

The trans-Atlantic voyage was long and arduous, but the family's trials did not end when they arrived in Quebec. From there, the group boarded a train to Toronto where they stayed in immigrant sheds for three days. Then they travelled to Collingwood, Ontario and boarded a steam ship to cross Lakes Huron and Superior.

Nelson Gerrard has reproduced a letter from one of the ship's passengers, Björn Andrésson, who tells of the voyage to Duluth, Minnesota:

> For days at a time no land was visible, and some even became seasick. The ship was very crowded and the cargo included sheep and cattle as well as passengers. Those occupying the area closest to these animals complained bitterly when the urine and manure from the pens ran into their quarters.[18]

Many years later, Elísabet reminisced during a newspaper interview "that they arrived by way of Glasgow, Scotland and Toronto, continuing on to Grand Forks, North Dakota. From there they travelled up the Red River by steamer to Winnipeg. Her favourite part of the journey was 'floating up the river to the mouth of Lake Winnipeg on barges. A little bit of a steamer towed all those barges from there to Gimli' […] It was June when the group left Iceland and October when they arrived at Gimli."[19]

Soon after the family's arrival in New Iceland, the community was hit with a smallpox epidemic that claimed the life of Elísabet's sixteen-year-old half-brother, Árni. Once again, Thuriður persevered, and established a homestead in the Árnes district, north of Gimli. It is the Icelandic tradition to name their farms, no matter how humble. The name Thuriður chose for her farm, *Melur*, reveals an ironic sense of humour. *Melur*, loosely translated, means "Sandy Ridge", and, perhaps not surprisingly, the farm was a total failure.

In 1879, Thuriður and her four surviving children moved to Winnipeg, but life there was also difficult. The family took up residence in a slum of scrap-lumber hovels called Shantytown, or the Icelandic Camp, near the forks of the Red and Assiniboine Rivers—but jobs were scarce, and Thuriður could barely make ends meet.

Thuriður eventually found work for herself and Elísabet as domestics in the home of a wealthy Winnipeg family. A life in service was a comedown for a proud and independent woman, but Thuriður did what she had to do to survive. However, there was still the question of what would become of her older children, who by now were almost adults.

At about this time, Thuriður discovered that Gísli, her former partner, had recently arrived from Iceland, and she sought him out in the hope of reuniting the family—but Gísli rejected her once again, saying that he intended to move to a new Icelandic settlement in Mountain, North Dakota (then known as *Vik*).

Gísli offered to take the older children with him, and two of them, Anna and Jóhann, took him up on the offer. Jóhann later moved again, this time to Seattle, Washington. Anna went on to live a rather itinerant life. She married twice, had two daughters and ended up operating a boarding house in Langruth, Manitoba from 1912 until shortly before her death in 1927.

Elísabet's other half-brother, Jón, who changed his name to John Anderson at some point, decided to stay in Manitoba. He would later establish a butcher shop at the corner of Portage Avenue and Smith Street, and settled in St. Andrews Municipality, just north of the city. Thuriður and Elísabet remained in service until Thuriður's death in April of 1888.

After his unhappy experience with Thuriður, Gísli decided that he preferred younger women. Sometime after settling in Mountain, he married a woman seventeen years his junior, and started another family. Young Elísabet visited her father from time to time, and maintained contact with his new family even after his death. Gísli's solicitude, however, did little to alleviate her shame over her illegitimacy, a burden that she would carry for the rest of her life. Gísli died in 1887, at the age of forty-five.

While life was never easy for the early Icelanders in Winnipeg, their circumstances did gradually improve over time. It was not long before the West End replaced Shantytown as the city's Icelandic ghetto, but, like many other immigrants before and since, the Icelanders were subjected to a degree of discrimination. The stereotypical Icelander has pale skin and fair hair, and someone had the idea that they looked like ghosts, or ghouls. As a result, Icelanders became known as ghoulies or goolies, and, ironically, were singled out because they were too white.[20]

In the mid-1880s, Elísabet met a stylish and gregarious young man named Ágúst Gunnarsson, who worked as a clerk in a local dry goods store. In an as yet unpublished manuscript, Nelson Gerrard writes of a friend's assessment of Ágúst as "a fun loving man with a joy for life and it was a pleasure to be in his presence and get to know him. He was witty and lively in conversation and told a wonderful story, especially jokes."

Ágúst's family had a somewhat scandalous history. Like Elísabet, he was born and raised in the Skagafjörður district of Iceland His grandmother, Helga Gottskálksdóttir, had been a beautiful young woman, and in 1829, at the age of 22, she went into service in the home of a 41-year-old clergyman, Rev. Ingjaldur Jónsson Reykjalín, and his wife. Helga became romantically involved with the pastor and in 1830, gave birth to Jóhanna, Ágúst's mother. The pastor acknowledged paternity, and continued his relationship with Helga who became pregnant with a second daughter. At that point, he and Helga ran off together, but the pastor later reconciled with his wife. In 1833, Helga, by now 26 years of age, was married off to Ingjaldur's first cousin, Ásmundur Einarson, who was three years her junior.

Despite its rocky start, Ásmundur and Helga had a successful marriage, although Ásmundur always resented being forced to raise another man's children, especially given that he and Helga had no children of their own. When disaster befell Iceland in the 1870s, Ásmundur and Helga, by now well into their sixties, set sail for Canada. (They were aboard the same ship as Elísabet and her family, a coincidence that would prove significant some years later.) It was agreed within the family that Helga and Ásmundur would take Helga's two eldest grandchildren, Ágúst's brother and sister, Jóhann and Pálina. They were also accompanied by Helga's nephew and his cousin, both thirteen years of age, who had also wanted to come to Canada but did not have the fare.

Ásmundur and Helga purchased their tickets as an act of charity, and a mutual bond of affection developed during the voyage. The boys referred to Ásmundur as their uncle, and he came to think of them as his nephews. After arrival in Manitoba, Ásmundur and Helga homesteaded near Winnipeg Beach for a short time and then established a farm just west of Gimli called *Hjarðarholt* or "The hill where the herd is kept". Jóhann and Pálina stayed with them, as did the two nephews who worked on the farm for several years. The two boys eventually settled in Winnipeg.

In 1879, Ágúst and his parents, Jóhanna and Gunnar, along with his younger brother, Snæbjörn, arrived, and their family was re-united. They stayed briefly at *Hjarðarholt* before the six of them took up residence in a small house in the West End of Winnipeg. Ásmundur and Helga remained on the farm, and lost touch with the rest of the family. Helga died in 1883.

By 1885, Pálina had married and started a family of her own. Jóhann was on the road, working for the railway. That winter, their father became disabled by either dementia or mental illness, and, by default, their brother, Ágúst became the household's breadwinner. (Gunnar died in 1904 at the "Home for the Incurables" in Portage la Prairie.)

Prior to meeting Ágúst, Elísabet's life had been one challenge after another. She had experienced deprivation both in Iceland and while living at *Melur*. She had witnessed the death of two siblings. She had been abandoned by her father, and later by two of her remaining siblings, and she had spent almost a decade in servitude as a child labourer. These struggles, however, helped to forge the formidable woman that the reader will come to know.

Happily, Ágúst gave no thought to Elísabet's illegitimacy, given that his own mother was also born out of wedlock. In 1888, just two months after her mother's death, 19-year-old Elísabet married the charming Ágúst in a ceremony performed by the Reverend Jón Bjarnason, the pastor of First Lutheran Church, the first Icelandic Lutheran congregation in Winnipeg. Elísabet moved in with Ágúst's family, and for the first time in a long time, felt part of a family.

As the turn of the century approached, the family had taken the name of Polson, an Anglicization of Ágúst's father's surname, Pálsson.[21] Elísabet was the mother of four children, and they were all still living in Ágúst's parents' home. By now, Ágúst's teenaged niece, Fjóla, daughter of his sister, Pálina, had also moved in, bringing the total of people living in the small house to nine. Quarters were so cramped that Archie had to sleep on a cot in the attic.

But things were about to change for Elísabet and her family. Elísabet would become known for her compassion and hospitality—and for good reason. Family legend has it that one warm spring day, her kind nature reaped an unexpected reward when she happened to meet Ásmundur Einarson while walking down the street one late afternoon. Elísabet's daughter, Florence, told the story to the writer and his brother, and she also made some notes that were discovered after her death.

Florence started by telling us about Ásmundur, and how he and Helga sponsored the two boys to come to Canada. She told us how Ásmundur grew close to his "nephews" during the voyage, and how that bond of affection strengthened during their time at *Hjarðarholt*.

The years passed, and eventually Ásmundur decided to retire from the farm and move in with relatives in Baldur, an Icelandic community in western Manitoba. By now over 80, long widowed and with no children of his own, he decided to give the farm to the two nephews.

So Ásmundur, almost unbelievably given his age, set out from Gimli on foot, and slept that night by the fire in an Indian camp. One would assume that somewhere along the way he was offered a ride, but, in any event, Ásmundur completed the ninety-kilometer trek to Winnipeg the following day, and went to visit his nephews. He had hoped one or the other of them would invite him to stay the night, but one had married a widow with two children and claimed, likely with justification, that he did not have room. The other nephew was living in a rented room, and likewise, could not accommodate the old man. Ásmundur was upset, perhaps unfairly, by what he believed to be a lack of hospitality, and decided against his proposed gift. He resolved to spend the night sleeping under a bridge.

By late afternoon, Ásmundur was wandering the streets of the West End when Elísabet came upon him. She recognized him immediately, despite not having seen him since their voyage from Iceland. Not surprisingly, Ásmundur did not recognize Elísabet at first. She introduced herself, and insisted that he come to her home. According to Florence's notes,

Ásmundur visited our place, and Mother asked him to stay for supper, and he could visit with Dad. During supper, Mother asked him where he was spending the night, and he didn't know as yet, and Mother said, 'That settles it! You can stay here.' He could not understand how she could make room for him when she had a houseful of people.

Elísabet arranged a makeshift bed of blankets on the floor for young Archie and the old man slept on Archie's cot in the attic. Ásmundur stayed for several days, and when it came time for him to leave, he told Elísabet of his plan to give his farm to his nephews, and his disappointment at their lack of hospitality.

He said he was grateful for all she had done for him, and that he had decided to give her the farm. And so, after some delays, the family, including Ágúst's parents, embarked on a new adventure with high hopes and great enthusiasm.

Ágúst was ill-suited to be a farmer. He soon found work in the Town of Gimli, but the family stayed on the farm. Florence wrote about life there:

The house was a two-storey whitewashed with calcimine. Mother made curtains with cheese cloth, frills and all, starched and prim. We were 2½ miles out in the country, west of Gimli. They had two cows, chickens, sheep, a dog, and one horse that Dad used to transport him to and from work. Dad had a hired man to look after the animals and do chores.

Life at *Hjarðarhol* was a big change from the City, but the children, especially Archie, loved it. The farmhouse was drafty and decrepit and relatively remote, given that there was no motorized transportation available. In 1905, Elísabet lost a child in childbirth, apparently due to their remote location,[22] which prompted the family to move into Town the following year. Florence Paulson wrote about this difficult time for the family.

We were on the farm only six years. The baby [...] died, and the doctor said that he felt that if he had more professional help, the baby would have lived. So we moved off the farm, and we were in the town from then on.[23]

Gimli is the Old Norse word for heaven or paradise, and Elísabet came to believe the town was aptly named. The people were friendly, and she had a houseful of happy children—she and Ágúst eventually had ten. The elder Polson children helped with the younger ones, but the two oldest, Josie and Bonnie, left home early, so the amiable Archie, still in his teens but adored by his younger siblings, became his mother's principal assistant in child rearing. The family also kept a menagerie of farm animals that they raised on the large property that they rented.

Ágúst found work as a clerk, and at the outbreak of World War 1 was employed by Sigurdson and Thorvaldson ("s&t") who operated general stores in various towns in the Interlake, principally Gimli and Riverton. Later he left s&t after he grew tired of being sent to work in their Riverton store, which he referred to as a "godforsaken place". He immediately accepted a position with Tergesen's Store of Gimli. The store was operated by H.P. Tergesen, known to most as "H.P."[24] Ágúst also worked part-time as the assessor for the Town of Gimli, for which he was paid $2.00 per day, and he served as a member of the local school board and town council.

An unexpected benefit to working for H.P. was the arrival of Margrét Gísladóttir as a member of the Polson household. Margrét, known in the family as Maggie, was H.P.'s widowed mother-in-law, and H.P. did not care for her. He asked Ágúst if she could work for the Polsons as a domestic in return for room and board. Maggie had worked in several homes before landing with the Polsons, but she felt most at home with them. She lived with the Polsons for a total of 23 years.

Ágúst's younger brother, Snæbjörn, or Snyder as he became known, and his family were frequent visitors to the Polson home, often for months at a time. Snyder was a gifted artist but he was also a ne'er-do-well and a dreamer. He had previously abandoned his family for two years to travel throughout the United States as an itinerant artist, supporting himself painting signs and shop windows. By the pre-war years, he had returned to his wife and family. Guðrun, also known as Núni or Noonie, was Snyder's wife, and Jóhanna was their daughter. Snyder was twelve years younger than Ágúst.

Ágúst's older brother, Jóhann Polson, was the most ambitious of the Polson brothers. He became active in the Liberal Party of Canada, and when the Liberal government of Wilfrid Laurier was elected in 1896, he was rewarded with a senior position in the federal Immigration Department in Winnipeg, with special responsibility for the Icelanders.

Jóhann was now a man of considerable influence, and he made the most of it. He and his wife Jónína, who called herself Nina (*Ny-na*), lived in a large house at 111 Rose Street[25] in Fort Rouge, a waspish and prestigious neighbourhood in the south end of Winnipeg. Jóhann died at the age of 49 in 1912, but Nina and their daughter, Dorothy, resided in Fort Rouge for the rest of their lives. After serving in World War 1, Jóhann's son, Frank Mulvey Polson[26] married an "English" girl and embarked on a career with The Great West Life Assurance Company.

Ágúst and Elísabet did not assimilate nearly so quickly, but the Christian names of the children reveal a family in transition from one culture to another. Almost all the names are either British or were informally anglicized. They were, from the eldest to the youngest: (1) Jóhanna, known as Josie; (2) Elizabeth Hazeltine, named after a character in a novel, and known as Bonnie; (3) Archibald John, the derivation of Archibald is unknown, but John was for Elísabet's half-brother, Jón, who went by John; (4) Florence Nightingale, named for the English nurse who became famous during the Crimean War; (5) Margrjét, also known as Margaret; (6) Robert Wyatt, who went by Wyatt, named for Ágúst's employer when they lived in Winnipeg; (7) Ágústa Sigríður Björg, known as Gústa; (8) Lena Byron, named for a friend of Elísabet; (9) Fjóla Alexandra, named for Ágúst's niece and Queen Alexandra of England, the wife of King Edward VII; (10) Jóhann Konráð, known as Konnie.

Florence,[27] whose married surname was Paulson, was instrumental in bringing this book to reality. Florence was a pack rat and kept much of Archie's early correspondence and many of his photos, including some Archie took with his own rudimentary camera. In addition, she made notes of the Polson family's life, some of which have already been cited.

By the late 1800s, Manitoba politics and commerce were controlled by Anglo-Saxon immigrants from Ontario, mostly Scots, who came in waves after Manitoba joined Confederation in 1870. The Icelanders and the immigrants from other European nations, the vast majority poor and with limited English language skills, had little choice but to work at menial jobs, and try to fit into this new society. The Icelanders were a highly literate people with a love of learning, but only the wealthy among them could afford to provide their children with more than a basic education.

One such child of wealthy parents was Lárus Sigurdson, a close friend of Archie, and the son of Johannes Sigurdson, a partner in the store where Ágúst was employed. Lárus graduated in medicine from the University of Manitoba in 1927, and later completed post-graduate studies in anatomy at Stanford University in California.[28] He also had a life-long association with the Polson family, serving as their family physician.

There would be no such fine education for Archie. Despite being a good student, he left school after Grade Ten in order to help with the family's finances. In the fall of 1911, Archie signed on with a fish merchant named J.H. Johnson to be the bookkeeper at a fish camp near Langruth, Manitoba, a predominantly Icelandic settlement on the west side of Lake

Manitoba.[29] In a letter home that he wrote on November 14th, 1911, he reported on his activities. At the outset of the letter, all appears fine, although Archie is unimpressed by his employer:

All the bookkeeping I have done is to write letters and bills and two accounts. I think I will get on alright although the boss's head is not quite level and [he's] apt to forget.

Later in the letter, it becomes clear that Archie was doing much more than bookkeeping:

Well, I was doing chores around camp and putting down nets until noon. After dinner, Johnson sent me out on the lake to set nets with two other fellows. At four o'clock, a fellow came to take my place and at 4:30 I went out with Dori Rosinkrantz to lift nets. We lifted three nets and got back to camp just as it was getting dark. We had a train of dogs and quite a load of fish.

Archie also included a rough sketch of his cramped sleeping quarters in the shack that he occupied with his fellow fishermen.

So Archie was an ice fisherman. Ice fishing in Manitoba is grueling work performed under difficult weather conditions. In those days, the job involved drilling holes in the ice using a manual augur, and setting gill nets between the holes with a spring-loaded device. Later, the nets were hauled out, and the fish are disentangled, piled on a sled and returned to camp where they were cleaned and packed into crates.

All of this was accomplished amid howling winds, occasional blizzards and ambient temperatures that reached as low as -40 C. From photos taken at the time, Archie appeared fine-boned and almost frail, and yet he was undeterred by his circumstances. In February of 1912, he sent a cheery hand-written birthday postcard to his sister Florence. He affixed the stamp upside down, an old sign of endearment.

FEB. 10, 1912

Dear Floss,

I hope this card will reach you before your birthday.
Many happy returns of the day to you Kiddo. I don't
know when I will be coming home. I think I will stick
to the job as long as it lasts. Be good to yourself and
turn over a new leaf on your birthday & quit your
mischief. A.P.

Florence would later write that Archie loved life on the lake, but added:

This was Archie's first and only time on the lake. He was supposed to do their
bookkeeping. Dad was afraid that if he was too interested in his work on the
lake, he would not want to go back to school.

So Archie returned home, and ultimately completed Grade Eleven, a good education for the son of immigrants. When World War I broke out, he was working as a labourer and delivery boy with his father at Sigurdson and Thorvaldson.

In February of 1916, Archie, by now twenty years of age, heard that a battalion had been formed in nearby Selkirk, Manitoba. Like Gimli, Selkirk was a fishing community with a large Icelandic population. This new battalion, known as the 108th, was put together by the local Member of Parliament, George Henry Bradbury, and was comprised almost entirely of Icelanders from the Interlake.

Archie's cousin, Frank Polson, with whom he was close, had enlisted with the Winnipeg Grenadiers. Archie would have done the same, but the 108th was to train near Gimli during the summer, and Archie's family wanted him nearby for as long as possible. So Archie signed up with the 108th.

For people like the Polsons, it was important to "fit in", which meant loyalty to Great Britain, and a willingness to serve "King and Country." It is not surprising therefore that Archie chose to enlist. It may have been that the decision was not entirely altruistic. The website of Library and

Archives Canada has this to say about the motivation of many young men in Archie's position:

> At the beginning of the First World War a wave of enthusiasm swept Canada; many Canadians felt a duty to enroll in the Canadian Expeditionary Force. With little military experience, most Canadians had never been involved in armed conflict. For many citizens, enrolling in the Canadian Expeditionary Force was considered a duty to their motherland, while others viewed it as an opportunity to earn a regular salary, to embark on a great adventure or to test their courage and moral fibre.[30]

Archie took his initial training at the 108th battalion's makeshift training ground established on a farm near Selkirk known as The Red Feather Farm. The battalion was barracked in chicken barns, and adopted the red rooster as an emblem which was emblazoned on their collars and hat badges. The summer training in Gimli never came to pass, and in mid-June the 108th was sent to Camp Hughes, in the western part of Manitoba—and the road to Archie's destiny began.

CHAPTER TWO

WE'RE IN THE ARMY NOW

ARCHIE'S LETTERS FROM CAMP HUGHES reveal his excitement at being a soldier. His cousin, Frank Polson, was also training there with his regiment, as well as another "cousin", a tall, sparely-built 42-year-old bachelor named Ásmundur Einarson.

Mundi, as Ásmundur was known (pronounced *Min-dee*), was apparently related to the man who gifted *Hjarðarholt* to Elísabet, so she referred to the younger Ásmundur as cousin or, in Icelandic, *frændi*. Icelanders traditionally adopt a liberal definition of the term "cousin". During the war, Mundi would act like an older brother to Archie.

Archie immediately began his correspondence with his mother. He often wrote his letters over a period of time, perhaps to save on postage. An early letter home was started on June 16, 1916 and finished on June 30. In the first portion of the letter, Archie goes to great lengths telling of the training he had undergone. He also included detailed sketches to show how the training exercises were conducted.

In the June 30th portion of the letter, Archie mentions having received a box of pancakes. Icelandic pancakes, called *pönnukökur*, are thin like a crepe. In their Canadian iteration, brown sugar is sprinkled on the *pönnukökur* which is then rolled up tight and eaten with the hands.

CAMP HUGHES
JUNE 16TH 1916
Dear Mother and Dad,
I was inoculated for the second time yesterday. I won't have another dose of it until I cross the ocean, or so I hear. It is about 11 o'clock A.M. now and I will

soon be having dinner. It was Tuesday June 6th when I got my first inoculation. On Wednesday (the day after) we did not drill. I believe that's the day I wrote to you last.

On Thursday my company ("C" company) or rather a part of it, went out to the rifle ranges. The rifle range is about a mile from here. We left Camp at 7 o'clock A.M. and stayed at the ranges until 5 o'clock P.M. when we came back to Camp. We had our dinner out there. We were setting up targets out there. The targets are arranged on posts which are stuck down in ten foot deep trenches. There are men in the trenches raising and lowering these targets. The target works on a hinge which when raised the target sticks up over the trench and when lowered is down in the trench out of sight of the men who are shooting at it.

The 108th were in the trench looking after the targets and the 101st Battalion were shooting at the targets. At first, they took their time at aiming and shooting, and after every shot we would take down the target to paste over the bullet hole. Then, when we put up the targets again we would show the shooters by signs where they hit last. There were two men looking after each target. One put the target up and down according to orders, and the other one pasted over the bullet holes and kept the score.

Another time, the shotsmen [sic] only got six seconds to get their aim and fire. The targets were raised all at the same time, and then lowered after six seconds. Another time the targets were up for thirty seconds, and in that time the gunners were to aim and fire five shots. The 101st were shooting that day and the scores were rather mixed. Some of them scored fairly well, and others scored rotten.

We targetmen [sic] had a rather easy time of it in the morning. The afternoon, however, was quite hot and we did not get any breeze in the trench. It was warm work. We were not in any danger because we did not go out of the trenches at all until dinner time. By that time, the shooting had stopped and no shooting was done until after dinner. We will go over there again someday soon, and then we'll do the shooting.

JUNE 23RD FORENOON

It was raining this morning and we did not drill at all. I don't know whether we will have to go out this afternoon or not. All depends on the weather I *guess. We were to go out to the rifle ranges to shoot but then I will have to go on guard to-night. It won't be very pleasant as it is raining hard.*

JUNE 30TH

Well, it is about 14 days since I started this letter and about eight days since I wrote the last addition to it. I went on guard duty last night and liked it all right. It will be quite a while before I have to go on guard again. The 108th Battalion went to the rifle ranges yesterday, and the day before yesterday, to see how well we could shoot and we did pretty well. We scored very high on an average, and I scored fairly well even if I do say so myself.

We had a general review today. The Duke of Connaught reviewed all the battalions in Camp Hughes. Sam Hughes was there I think and some big bug by the name of Sifton. It was some grand parade. Everybody was dressed up and polished to perfection, and all marched their very best. I have got paid up to the end of this month.

I got $50.00 the first payday and $21.90 the last payday. I will send you as much as I can pretty soon. I am in too much of a hurry to do it now. I heard that some of the Gimli girls were coming to Camp Hughes on July 1st. That is to say tomorrow. We are all feeling well. Dennis Lee, Joe Daniel and Barney Viborg are back again. Those three took a holiday without a pass or permission, but did not get much punishment. It was certainly worthwhile for them to skip. The men who can't get passes are taking a pass on their own hook. They just catch a freight train in the middle of the night and come back when they feel like it. They keep on skipping all the time.

It is not the battalion commander's fault. It's the staff officers of the Camp who have to sign the passes. No private is allowed more than a week end pass. Even [Battalion Lieutenant-Colonel George] Bradbury has to get a pass and the same with all the lieutenant-colonels and all the officers.

I am going to apply for a pass in July, either the 8th or the 15th. There are all kinds of rumours about when we will leave for England. Sometimes, they say July 15th, but you can't believe a word you hear about it.

In some of the letters that the men get from their wives, they say that Winnipeg people talk about how badly we're treated in Camp Hughes. And they are the awfulest lies you ever heard. We have no kick coming except for the passes.

I got a letter and a box of pancakes from Guðrun Danielsdottir and I treated the boys to pancakes. Joe Daniel got his box from home all right and I got my stuff okay.

I kept the tarts for myself and Mundi and Frank and treated the boys to the cookies or the cookies to the boys. There are quite a bunch of ladies and civilians here on Saturday afternoons and Sundays. It's rather a novelty to see a woman here.

I wish you would send this letter to Bonnie when you have read it and then Bonnie can send it to [name apparently nibbled by a mouse] I can't write long letters to everybody. Give my best regards to all the friends and love to all the family.

With love from Archie.

P.S. I am going to start another letter soon because it takes me so long to finish one. Don't feel worried though you don't get a letter often. I won't keep anything from you that you should know. I am getting along fine.

Don't forget to give my best regards to Miss Stjana Orr and ask her to write. Tell her how little time I have to write. She promised to write to me. Tell her I will write to her very soon.

[Icelandic] Mundi sends his greetings. He is so very useless at writing.

Archie.

Archie's report on the general review of the battalion by the Governor-General, the Duke of Connaught, as well as by Sir Sam Hughes and "a big bug named Sifton" is of particular interest. Hughes was the federal Minister of the Militia and Camp Hughes was named for him. He and the Duke of Connaught, who was the younger brother of King George v, hated each other. Historian Ronald Haycock has documented their rift in his biography of Hughes:

> On the night of October 12th, 1911, the Empress of Ireland bearing the new Governor-General, the Duke of Connaught, docked at Quebec City.

Grey, the departing head of state, secretly came aboard to give the Royal Prince his private reservations about Mr. Borden's six-day-old government. No doubt these frank comments included substantial reservations about Hughes as Militia Minister. Whatever else transpired between the two aristocrats, Connaught was not long in portraying Sam Hughes as "an impossible fellow ... eaten up with conceits and ... very ignorant in military matters." For his part, Hughes claimed that on the day he landed in Canada Connaught had snubbed the Minister and other members of the Militia Council. Clearly their relationship did not get off to a good start, and it did not take long to deteriorate further.[31]

The "Grey" to which reference is made is Albert Henry George Grey, the 4th Earl Grey, the outgoing Governor-General of Canada.[32]

Given the state of the relationship between Hughes and Connaught, one can imagine the icy chill between the two men at the ceremony. The "big bug name of Sifton" was Sir Clifford Sifton who had been the Minister of the Interior in Prime Minister Sir Wilfrid Laurier's Liberal government. Sifton was largely responsible for the great surge in immigration of which the Icelanders were a part. He retired in 1911, and the fact that Archie's battalion was made up almost entirely of Icelanders may have been a factor in his being invited to attend.

Archie refers to Miss Stjana Orr at the close of the letter. While Archie had many friends who were girls, Kristjana Orr, Stjana for short, was his girlfriend. While Archie mentioned her from time to time in his letters home, their correspondence has not been found.

Camp life was not always easy, as is evident in Archie's next letter. He reported on a torrential rainstorm that hit Camp Hughes. There is also an indication near the end of the letter that the soldiers, Archie included, were growing tired of camp life, and people were getting testy.

CAMP HUGHES
JULY 7TH 1916
Dear Mother,
I received your welcome letter, and was glad to get it and the tickets. I did not get a pass this week end. I transferred to the Machine Gun Section Tuesday

and started learning machine gun drill and signals etc. on Wednesday. There were two of us transferred out of our platoon, Swany Johnson and I.

Our Major was sorry to have us go out of "C" company. We tried once before to get a transfer to the M.G.S. [Machine Gun Section] but our Major would not let us. He does not want to lose any men out of his company. But this time he could not stop us. The M.G.S. needed men and Bradbury told the Lieutenant of the M.G.S. that he could take men out of any company in the battalion.

I had asked for a pass before I left "C" company but we did not get it. I guess it was because the major would not recommend it for I know he was sore at us for leaving him. I am going to apply for one again for Saturday 15th. The boys tell me that I stand a better chance of getting one in the M.G.S. I went to two shows tonight and feel tired. I think I'll quit for tonight as the mosquitoes are pretty bad.

GOOD-NIGHT.

SUNDAY MORNING, JULY 9TH, 10 A.M.

Dear Mother,

I am just back from church parade and as it is about two hours to dinner time, I think I will continue this letter. We had an awful storm out here last Thursday as you may have read in the papers. We had just fallen in for parade at 8 o'clock Thursday morning and the sky was pretty black, and it kept turning blacker. The officers saw the storm coming and dismissed the battalion. Just after we reached our tents, it started to blow hard from the north. Then it blew something fierce, so it was hard to stand on our feet. It blew clouds of dust over us. The cloud of dust was just like the worst snow storm I ever saw. The dust was so thick and flying so fast that you could only see a short distance away.

Then the rain came down in tankfuls. It came down as if a high pressure hose had been turned on us. Everybody hung onto their tents for dear life to keep them from blowing over. I had transferred to the Machine Gun Section the day before and I was sleeping with the M.G.S. boys the night before. Some of our tent pegs got pulled up, but we managed to hold the tent down. The tent next to ours got blown down and the poor fellows got soaked to the skin and all their stuff got soaken [sic]. Not many of the smaller tents got blown down but most of the large ones did.

The band tent, the sergeants' mess, the quarter master stores tent and the paymaster all got blown down, and several others. Our canteen is a frame building with a canvas roof and it withstood the storm all right, but the canteens of some of the other battalions were just in tents, and many of them blew down. The officers' kitchen was flooded with water because it was on low ground, and we had to dig ditches to get the water away. It is an easy matter to drain water out here. All you have to do is to dig a one-foot-deep trench in the ground, then you strike sand and the water sinks into the sand like water into a sponge. It did not take long to get things into shape again.

In the afternoon the ground was nearly all dry, and the men's clothes were dry and the tents were all up. The storm and rain lasted only a little over an hour, and the sun was shining bright at noon. But it certainly was dark just before the rain. It was just like 10 o'clock at night. I got pretty well soaked too. I went out in the rain to fasten down the tent pegs so the tent wouldn't go down. However, I did not catch cold or anything like.

Just after the storm was over I went digging drain trenches with wet clothes on because I did not have time to change. The boys were not downhearted at all. They were all cheerful as could be and thought it was a great joke. I haven't seen Frank [Polson] for quite a while. The last time I saw him I went over there and gave him some of the tarts that you had sent to me. He has only come to see me once since he came. I was downtown, and I met him on the way back. I have been to see him often, and once or twice when I went there I could not find him anywhere. Once when I went to see him he was in Winnipeg on pass. I am going over to see him today.

It is quite a long way to go. Frank is too darned lazy to walk all that way. If I was to depend on him to come over, I would never see him. We are at the very west end of the Camp and he is at the very east end. I wrote a letter to Bonnie the other day and I am going to try to get up enough energy to write to Josie. It is tiresome work writing letters.

All the boys find it that way. It is alright to receive letters, and I guess that a fellow has got to write once in a while if he expects to get letters from others.

All the Icelanders are well. Mundi is grouchy most of the time because he did not get all his pay last pay day. It's the same old story with him. He was getting to be tiresome to be with for a while. I don't see him so very often these days since I transferred because I have been busy during my spare time washing my clothes. I don't send any of it to the laundry except the woolen underwear which is so hard to wash.

GOOD-NIGHT.

Love
Archie.

CHAPTER THREE

SEE CANADA FIRST

AT LAST THE BOYS WERE ON THEIR WAY. On September 9, Archie wrote to Elísabet to tell her that he was shipping out shortly, and assumed that she would travel to Winnipeg to see him. He also made a rather pragmatic request.

CAMP HUGHES,
SEPT. 9TH, 1916.
Dear Mother,
I am writing this in a hurry. It is nearly 9 o'clock Saturday evening, and I must catch the mail. We are leaving Camp at 10 o'clock next Tuesday, Sept. 12th. That is the latest news.

We will pass through Winnipeg about 2 o'clock Wednesday morning. I wish you would get me a couple of pairs of good hand-knit wool socks. Good night, dear Mother.

Your loving son,
Archie.

The next series of letters is actually a serial letter written in several installments over the period of September 14 to October 9. Archie reported on his trip across Canada, on the way to England. He was having a wonderful time. Gone was the boredom of Camp Hughes, and in its place an unexpected opportunity to see the country.

Archie even made a stop at the Parliament buildings, where Prime Minister Robert Borden addressed the troops. Archie tried to capture what he witnessed for the folks back home.

He then went on to tell us about his voyage across the Atlantic, settling into Witley Camp, and finally, his first visit to London.

SOMEWHERE IN ONTARIO
SEPT. 14TH 1916

Dear Mother,

This looks like a drunken man's writing. I am writing this on the train, and it rocks so much that I can hardly write at all. We are somewhere in Ontario about three hundred miles east of Port Arthur [Thunder Bay]. It is 8.30 P.M. Ontario time, which is one hour faster than Winnipeg time. I opened up some of my parcels Tuesday night, exploring the contents. Then I went to sleep.

When I woke up about six o'clock in the morning, I looked out the window and saw some pretty scenery. The first station we went past in the morning was "Malachi." There were only a station and two or three houses situated on the shore of a tiny lake. I don't feel like writing any more tonight but will continue in the morning. I don't feel lonesome at all, and I know that I am going to get along fine.

Good night dear mother,
Your loving son,
Archie.

ON THE TRAIN SOMEWHERE EAST OF NORTH BAY, ONT.
SEPT. 15TH 1916 (FRIDAY)

Dear Mother,

It is about eleven o'clock in the morning. We stopped at North Bay about an hour ago, but did not go out of the train at all. Day before yesterday (Wednesday) we stopped at Graham for about an hour and a half, and the major took us out for a short route march. We only marched about one mile. Graham is somewhere west of Fort William. We have just gone past a station called Alderdale. It is not much of a place. There are only a few houses there. Yesterday we stopped at a station called Hornepayne. We caught up to the train which the first bunch of the 108th are on.

They were filling the train tanks with water. By that, I mean the engine was taking on water and the train men were filling the drinking water tanks in the coaches. I'm sorry if my grammar is poor, and my statements are not very clear. I am not exactly in a mood for writing, but I must write before I forget what I have seen. While passing through new scenery a person is apt to forget for the moment the other scenery and places he has already seen.

We are at the present passing along a ridge. On one side, there is just bush and on the other side, there is a valley. Beyond the valley is a high hill, and more hills in the distance. On the nearest hill there is a farmer ploughing a field up and downhill. Of course by the time I have written this we are several miles past that place.

I would be pretty busy if I were to write about every change of scenery we have passed through. Now I think I have wandered from what I was going to tell you. We caught up to the other train at Hornepayne. The boys out of the other train were marched past our train and back again. Then we were marched past their train and back again. I saw most of the boys that I know, but did not have time to speak as we marched past. Only could say "Hello", but we were glad to have a chance to say even that, even though we have been separated such a short time.

We have passed many pretty scenerys [sic], but we are getting fed up on it. We want to see a little bit of civilization. I know that this writing looks kind of sea sick. The train rocks so much I can hardly write. It is lots of fun trying to see how well you can write when the train is rocking.

We have just passed a small lake surrounded by wooded hills. The trees are kind of mixed. There is birch, hemlock, tamarac [sic], etc. The lake was narrow and the train goes over it on a bridge. It is supper time now and I think I'll go and eat.

In the meantime,

Be Good.

I have been wondering whether this is regular Ontario weather we are having now. It rained last night but it hasn't rained at all today, but still the weather has been dull and dark. I was writing this letter just before dinner and when I left off writing you will no doubt notice that I wrote that I was going to supper but it was only dinner time and it was dinner I ate. The train has just stopped at some little one-horse town to get water I guess, and I am going to make use of the stop so as to write. The name of this place is Ellis or Alice or something like that. The boys were saying that our next stop will be Pembroke. The worst of this journey is we don't see any good-sized towns. We have only struck three good-sized towns in all these hundreds of miles. The only towns we passed that were of any size were Fort William, Port Arthur and North Bay.

We passed Fort William and Port Arthur about midnight Wednesday, and I was sound asleep. We have gone through miles and miles of wilderness, and the stations that we have passed have consisted mostly of two or three houses, and the stations have been few and far between. We are all longing for the sight of civilization.

It seems that this C.N.R. misses all the big towns of Ontario. We have been going through the backwoods alright. We passed a few farmhouses just now for a wonder. I saw about half a dozen cattle a while ago. They are the first cattle I have seen since we came to Ontario. We have just left the station called Alice, and the train is going at a pretty good rate, so my handwriting will be looking groggy again. It is supper time now and I think I'll go and eat. I'm not making any mistake about which meal I'm going to eat this time.

ON THE TRAIN A FEW MILES EAST OF RIVIÈRE DE LOUP.
PROVINCE OF QUEBEC
SUNDAY MORNING
SEPT 17TH 1916:
Dear Mother,
I was just thinking that I must continue this letter and tell you about some of the pretty scenery we have passed. Rivière de Loup is a pretty French town. It is quite large, and has some pretty buildings in it. We stopped at the station there about fifteen minutes, but we could not see much of the town from there. After we got past the station, we had a good view.

The train goes along a hill around the outskirts of the town, and the town is situated between the hill and the St Lawrence River. It sure is a pretty view from the train. The other side of the river is very hilly, right to the water's edge. It is very rocky country. The hills on the other side look as if they are solid rock.

Just as I write this, I have another view of the river. The train has been traveling about three-quarters of a mile from the river, but at present we are close to it. I can see a small island in the river and a boat on the river.

The river is very wide here, and there is a mist on the river, and the hills on the other side are not distinct. The river looks like a long and narrow lake. We have just passed some beautiful scenery. I only wish I had a camera to take some pictures. I sure could have taken some pretty pictures. I have noticed along the river that some of the people gather some kind of seaweed or river grass from the banks of the river. They scatter it on dry land so it will dry. I think they use it for fodder.

I am going to start writing on both sides of this note paper. If I don't, I will have an awful bunch of paper to mail home. I will hardly be able to get it into an envelope.

We have lost sight of the river now. There is a high, steep, rocky hill between it and us. We may be quite a distance from it now for all I know. These rocky hills look pretty (very much so). They are very steep and rocky, and the trees that grow on them are scattered in small clumps.

The farmers around here seem to make use of every bit of ground that can be used for farming. The whole country is fenced in long, narrow strips of lands. All the way from Quebec, the farms have been long narrow strips and everyone has been fenced in and all the fences have been rail fences. We have just stopped at a little town called St. Fabien. I don't know how long we stay here. We are to have a route march today at two o'clock but I don't know in what town. It is dinner time now and I think I'll go and eat.

3.30 P.M. SUNDAY

We are somewhere east of Petit Métis now. At noon we went past Sacré Coeur. Since then we have passed Rimouski, Mont Joli and Petit Métis in the province of Quebec. We had a half-hour's march at Mont Joli. We marched around town a little, and then went back to the cars.

Well, I think I'll tell you about our stay in Ottawa. We came to Ottawa the night before last, just about midnight, and we stayed in the cars that night. Yesterday morning at nine o'clock, we marched down to the Parliament

Buildings to have our colours presented to us. We were presented with our colours with great ceremony. Borden made a speech and we were praised to the skies for neatness and for being a sturdy looking bunch of men. There were many military staff officers (you know these officers with their caps and coat lapels trimmed with red). Then we marched back to the train. We did not stay there very long.

Two days later, Archie and his comrades in the 108th Battalion boarded the *Olympic* in Halifax. The *Olympic* was a renowned ocean liner, one of the White Star Line's trio of Olympic-class liners that included the *Titanic* and the *Britannic*. Except for the brief careers of its two slightly-larger sister ships, the *Olympic* was the largest ship in the world from 1911 until 1934 when the *Queen Mary* was launched. Referred to as "Old Reliable", the RMS *Olympic* made ten round trips from Halifax to Liverpool between March and December 1916, usually carrying 6,000 troops at a time.

The 108th arrived in Liverpool on September 25, and the troops were immediately transported to Camp Witley, where Archie continued his marathon letter. It had now been almost two weeks since he started it. He described his first few days in England and his ocean voyage.

Archie refers to being "downtown every night". The nearest town to Witley Camp is Chiddingfold. It is the site of The Crown Inn, one of the oldest inns in England. The Crown Inn dates back to as early as 1285, and includes an alehouse, where Archie and his friends likely spent some time.

WITLEY CAMP, ENGLAND
SEPT. 27TH 1916
Dear Mother,
We arrived in Witley Camp night before last. We did not know that we would come to this Camp until we were on the ship. The Camp is situated in a woody spot, and is very pretty. We sleep in frame buildings, thirty men in each building, and we have plenty of room and comfortable beds. The baths and some of the other buildings are built of brick. We eat our meals in a big dining room.

The meals we get are alright, or at least what we have got so far. The grub we get here is every bit as good and about as much as we got in Camp Hughes.

We have not done any drilling as yet. We have been fixing things up and settling down. We sleep on little bunks about eight inches off the floor. This bunk consists of two low trestles with three boards laid across them. The boards are about 10 inches wide each. These bunks make a fairly comfortable bed.

We had a fine voyage on the ocean. We had calm weather all the way, and I did not hear of any one getting sea sick. We had a good time on the ship. The machine gun section had good quarters on the steam ship. Many of the soldiers had to sleep down below in the dining room, and it was very close and stuffy there at night. The M.G.S. were up on deck on the starboard side on the fifth deck, and we had plenty of fresh air up there.

WITLEY CAMP, SEPT. 30TH.

We are pretty well settled down now. I have been downtown every night since I came. I went downtown with Ásmundur last night. He seems to like this place alright. The towns around here are pretty close together. There are three around here, and they look as if they were all one town. There is a string of houses and shops between them. I can't tell where one town starts or where it ends. We drilled yesterday and day before. The ground we have to drill on is not very good. It is very rough.

There are two Alberta battalions here. The 138th battalion from Edmonton is in this Camp. That is the battalion that Oscar Gottskalkson [Archie's cousin] belongs to. I am going to look him up one of these days. The 100th is in Camp here also. I have not gone to see Frank yet. I was on a march with the battalion the day before yesterday and we went past where the 100th Signalers were signaling. I saw Frank, but could not speak to him.

WITLEY CAMP, OCT. 9TH
MONDAY

Dear Mother,

I have been to London, "where the streets are paved with gold" as they say. Half the battalion got a pass from Monday night until Sunday, but I was broke by Friday and came back that night.

I had three pounds with me, and I had a good time while they lasted. I went through the Tower of London and to the Zoological Gardens and several other places of interest. They say that London is altogether different now to what it was in time of peace, and I am sure of that. I came back to Camp as soon as I ran out of money, but I know that many of the boys stayed there after they were broke, and got along for a couple of days somehow or other.

I was glad to get back to Camp, that is to say, in a way. If I had had more money, then I certainly would have stayed. I am looking forward to my next pass to London, though I expect that it will be quite a while before any of us get another pass. I will know my way around the city better next time. We found it pretty hard this time, being perfect strangers.

The Machine Gun Section went on pass with "A" and "B" companies. "C" and "D" companies are going on pass tonight. The boys from down home will go on pass tonight. Mundi wanted to go with me to London, but we did not get our passes at the same time. The Fort Garry Horse are here in Camp, and Mr. Sherlock is in Camp with them so I heard. I am going to look him up pretty soon. You know he was Josie's neighbour.

We heard that the ship we came on has been reported sunk [an erroneous report]. It was said that the news of the sinking of our ship has been received in Canada. I was just wondering whether it had come out in the Canadian newspapers. I knew that if you heard such news, you would be worried.

This is getting to be a long letter, and I have been a terrible long time writing it and I am ashamed to think how long I have delayed sending this letter. But when it gets to you it sure is some letter. I can't write a letter like this to all the relatives and friends, so I think that you should kind of pass it around, or else have it copied. I don't think there is anything very personal in it. I received letters from you and the girls today. I got it all right and it was not opened at all. I sure was glad to get them. I hope you will write often. The letters you wrote were a long time coming.

You wrote them Sept. 17th and I got them today, Oct. 19th. I am going to leave off now. Give my love to all the folks and friends and be sure and remember me to old Maggie. Let her know that I haven't forgotten her yet.

Kiss Dad and all the kiddies for me. Tell Dad that this letter is to him as well as to you although I address it to you. Good bye and God bless you dear Mother and Dad.

Your Loving son Archie
Private A.J. Polson 721948, M.G.S. 108th Battn
C.E. T. Witley Camp
Godalming, Surrey, Eng.

P.S. I can imagine the excitement at home when you get this letter.

Here Archie finished the letter, and finally sent it.

CHAPTER FOUR

OH, TO BE IN ENGLAND

Witley Camp, known formally as Witley Military Camp, was a temporary army camp set up on Witley Common, Surrey, England, during both the First and Second World Wars. It did not take Archie long to tire of the place. He missed his family and friends, and he was broke after his trip to London. When Archie enlisted, he assigned a significant portion of his pay to his mother and father, but now that he was overseas, he often found that he was short of funds.

WITLEY CAMP
OCT. 11TH, 1916
Dear Mother and Dad,
I received your welcome letter today, together with a letter from Margaret [Archie's sister]. I was very glad to get it. I have just sent you a long letter. I'm afraid that you will be longing for a letter a long time before you get either of my letters. It takes about two weeks for the letters to go between Canada and England.

At least, that is what your letters took to reach me. That may have been on account of them going through the Army Post Office. Perhaps they will get here sooner when you address it direct to the Camp. It sure is good to hear from home, even though there wasn't much news in the letters I have received so far. I don't like to see the other boys get letters when I don't get any. A short letter with little news is better than none at all.

When all my friends start writing to me, I guess that I'll get more letters. But then I will have to write quite a few letters myself if I am to get letters from others. You were talking about sending me a parcel. It would be nice to get something good to eat from home. The food we get is fairly good, and if it does not get any worse, then I won't complain. The food is just about as good as what we got in Canada, except the bread is not nearly as good. It is so heavy, and I don't know why it is, but that's how it is. We never get tea at noon, but get soup instead.

Sending food to me is all right, but I would prefer cakes or tarts that you could very well send. I need money more than anything else. The trip to London broke me financially. When I came back I had to borrow a couple of shillings to keep me in cigarettes until pay day. We could not help spending money fast in London.

Everything is so dear there, especially food. I have only bought one meal in Camp since I came here. You must not think, dear mother, that I spend my money carelessly. I try to keep away from bad company, that is to say, I don't share their bad habits.

I know that there are some lads in the M.G. Section who you don't care much for, but I keep out of their company when they go on a spree. I have been with Mundi quite a lot since we came to Camp. He doesn't seem to associate very much with the boys in "C" Company, and he wants to be with me when I go downtown. I know he would help me out with money if I needed it, but I don't like to keep on borrowing from him. He lent me three dollars when we left Camp Hughes (which you knew about) and I have not been able to pay him back.

If I had paid him last pay day, I would not have been able to go to London and I wouldn't have missed that for anything. I had eight dollars coming to me last pay day, and I got $10.00 instead $8.00 because I was going to London. They gave everybody a little in advance when they went to London. I guess I will get so much less next pay day. I heard some talk about them holding back $5.00 a month for six months to have in case we come back from the front. Of course, I don't know whether there is any truth to it or not.

I would like very much if you could send me ten dollars. I know you need all you have, and I don't like to owe anybody any money. I have enough clothes, I think, to see me through for quite a while. But there are always some odd articles a fellow has to get. Well, dear mother, I guess this is enough talk about money. It is not a pleasant thing to worry about. I hope I won't have to ask you again. There is not much news to tell. We keep on pegging along at our drill, and the work is not very hard yet, whatever it may be later on.

The boys in "C" Company are all on pass now, and I suppose they are seeing many of the places that I have already seen. I guess I will finish this letter. I hope this will find you all in good health. Give my best regards to all the friends and love to the relatives. Kiss all the children for me and remember me to old Maggie.

Your loving son,
721948 Pte. A.J. Polson
M.G.S. 108th Battn C.E.F.
Witley Camp, Godalming, Surrey, Eng.

Almost a month went by before Archie wrote again. It turned out to be another of his serial letters. He was now separated from his cousins, Frank and Mundi. His views on girls, education and marriage are rather interesting.

Archie mentions having seen two copies of *Lögberg*. *Lögberg* was one of two Icelandic-language newspapers published in Winnipeg at the time, the other named *Heimskringla*. Some years later, the papers merged to become *Lögberg-Heimskringla*, a tongue-twister for non-Icelanders.

WITLEY CAMP
NOV. 3, 1916
Dear Mother,
I guess it will be near my birthday when you get this letter. It takes an awful long time for the letters to travel between us. I received a letter from you and Lena yesterday, and was glad to get them. I have now received four letters from home, and one from Bonnie. I have not received an answer to the letters I wrote home, but I know I will get them in two or three days. The letters will start coming in more regular after this.

The 108th Battalion left yesterday for another Camp at a place called Seaforth. The 100th and 144th went also. They all left their Machine Gun

Sections behind, so we are still here. We will be put in a Machine Gun Company or Brigade. At present, we are attached to the 107th for food and shelter until we go to the M.G. Training Camp. I did not like to leave the boys in "C" Company, but I think I will like this M.G. Brigade. I have heard that machine gunners are well treated in this country. We will have a lot to learn, and I am sure the work will be interesting.

I saw Frank the other night and said goodbye to him. He went with his battalion. I said goodbye to Mundi, and he said that whenever I write home he sends his best regards to you all. Is old Maggie still working for you? Tell her I send her my best regards. I suppose she will like to hear that I wanted to be remembered to her.

I was glad to hear that the people down home have enough sense to get married. Or would you call it "sense" or perhaps the opposite? I'll be darned if I know which it is. Some girls grow up to be wives; some grow up to be educated; some grow up and get educated, and then when they are educated they get married and raise kids. Of course, the girls that got married at Gimli lately were not very educated—but Karin is not married yet, is she? I don't want to marry her myself, but still I think she is too good for Hannes. He may be alright in a way, but still he is not the kind of a man I would want any of my sisters to marry. I do not have a very high opinion of him.

SUNDAY, NOV. 4TH

We have had an easy day today. It rained today and we stayed in our hut. Of course we never drill on Sunday, but we did not even go to church parade as our sergeant went on pass yesterday. We did not do much work yesterday either, just went on a short route march yesterday morning.

I would like you to send me some copies of the Red Book Magazine, beginning with the September number. I also asked Dad to send me some tobacco, Old Chum smoking tobacco. I guess he told you about it. Very likely you will have sent a parcel before you receive this letter. If you are in doubt about what to send me, I would like some cake, tarts, and home-made candy or toffee.

You might also send me some cigarettes, say two or three packages, and Old Chum tobacco. I need the Old Chum tobacco more than I do the cigarettes here, but not any kind of Canadian smoking tobacco. I don't like any of the English smoking tobacco. If I could get good smoking tobacco, I would smoke a pipe once in a while.

I am pretty well supplied with socks, but you might send me a pair of good woolen socks, although not more than one pair until I let you know that I need more. I have enough mitts. I hardly ever wear gloves, except just once in a while, and I guess I won't wear mitts until about Christmas time. I need letters and news from home most of all. I have only seen one copy of the Free Press since I came here, and about two copies of Lögberg.

Mundi and I were downtown to have coffee and cakes one evening and he said that he wished that he was at Mrs. A.G. Polson's house, having coffee and pancakes.

Well mother, pretty soon I will be twenty-one years old, and I guess it will be the second birthday that I have celebrated away from home. I don't think I will have much of a birthday party, but if I get letters from home just before or after my birthday, then I will be satisfied. Gústa's birthday will be on Dec. 13th if I am not mistaken, and I wish her many happy returns of the day, and the same to Lena.

Somehow I have an idea that Lena's birthday is on Nov. 8th. Tell her I will think of her on her birthday. And Konnie's birthday is on January 11th and Florence's on February 25th and yours in April or March and Fjóla's in May and Margaret's and Dad's in July, Bonnie's in August, Wyatt's and Josie's in October. I'm not very well posted on the birthday dates. Tell Konnie that I will write to him on his birthday, and also at Christmas. I will write to everyone of you at Christmas.

I will not write much more this time. Will write again soon. I don't know how long we will stay in this Camp, so you had better address letters after this to Army Post Office. Give my love to all the friends. Remember me to Miss Emma Thompson. Kiss Dad and the children for me.

Your Loving son,
#721948 Pte. S. J. Polson
M.G.S. 108th Battn C.E.F.
Army Post Office
London

Shortly after writing that letter to his mother, Archie was transferred to Crowborough Camp for machine gun training. Crowborough is in East Sussex, about fifty miles south of London. For the first time in the letters, Archie reflected on his decision to enlist. While he expressed no regrets, the fact that he chose to mention it at all may be revealing of his innermost thoughts.

There is a reference as well to Mr. Bristow's sister. Herbert Bristow was the Polsons' neighbour in Gimli. He was a British immigrant settled in Gimli, and became a fisherman on Lake Winnipeg. Herbert married an Icelandic woman, and he and his family resided across the road from the Polson house.[33]

Herbert left England under a cloud. Only sixteen years old at the time, he rebelled against his father, a prominent clergyman, and departed for Canada.

Two of his sons (the Bristows had thirteen children altogether) drowned in 1916, along with three other young people. Their sailboat capsized on Lake Winnipeg while they were returning from a berry-picking expedition to Hecla Island, north of Gimli. The boys were close friends of Archie, and the Polsons were particularly helpful to the Bristows in their time of loss.

Despite his differences with his father, Herbert maintained good relations with his nine siblings in England, among them Margaret Cecilia Tyler. When it became clear that Archie—and another friend of Herbert's boys named Pete Olson—would spend time in England, Herbert contacted his sister and asked her to invite Archie and Pete to visit her family, and to make them feel welcome.

Margaret had married into a prosperous family in Somerset, in the southwest corner of England. She and her husband ran a general store in the village of Highbridge. Archie visited her twice, once before going to France, and once just before his scheduled return to Canada. Mrs. Tyler would assume an ever-increasing role in Archie's life. Archie bonded with Mrs. Tyler and her family. He also made several friends while in Highbridge, including at least one young lady.

CROWBOROUGH, SUSSEX

NOV. 12TH 1916

Dear Mother,

I am writing this in the Y.M.C.A. I wrote a letter to my sister Lena last night. This is Sunday and I had to work all day on fatigue work in the quarter-master's stores. There were ten out of our section working there. The three sections who have come here (100, 108 and 144) have had their share of guard duty and fatigue work these three days since we have been here.

Things will be getting better though after a while. I suppose you will be sending me a parcel for Christmas, and if you do I would like you to send me about four or five plugs of McDonalds chewing tobacco. Several of the boys in the section chew tobacco, and it is impossible to get the kind of tobacco that they like here. I would like to be able to give them a good chew on Christmas. I expect to still be here at Christmas, and we all get six-day passes. I wish that you would send me some money for Christmas if you can, so I will have some money when I go on pass. The only fun a soldier gets here is when he goes on pass.

Well, Dear Mother, I have not received a letter from home in answer to the letters I wrote, but I am sure I will get one soon. I know that there must be some letters on the way. It may take the letters longer to reach me here since we moved as you have likely addressed them to Witley Camp. I have not heard from any of the boys of the 108th since they went to Seaford, but I wrote a letter to Ásmundur last night and let him know where I am.

It is not very cold here yet, but I guess it is getting rather cold back home in Manitoba. It has not rained much these last few days for which I have been thankful. It is very annoying when it rains, and the rain makes a fellow feel miserable. I have not been sick since I came here. I have only had a slight cold which was a running of the nose, but not coughing. I think I will get along fine.

We boys sometimes find the army life to be tiresome, but still I don't think we would want to be out of it. It is just the same with us here as in civil life; we are not always satisfied with our positions in civilian life either. The boys have a saying that, "We haven't got much money, but we do see life."

They are having a Divine service here in the Y.M.C.A. while I sit here writing to you, and the sermon is being delivered. They have just sung, "Abide with Me." When they started on the Lord's Prayer, I stopped writing, and joined in.

I have been thinking that you will be thinking of me on my birthday, just as I will be thinking of home. I wouldn't mind being home, but we are fighting for a good cause, and I wouldn't miss it for anything. I would not like to be sitting at home knowing that I had not tried to do my bit for my country, unlike some of the boys back there.

You must not think for a moment that I regret that I joined the army. I would do the same thing over again if I was still a civilian at home. But still home is "Home Sweet Home" to me and to all the boys who are away from home. I don't know where I will be at Christmas. I am sure that I will be in England, but I don't think I will be in Camp if I can possibly get a pass. I might go to London. Wherever I will be, my thoughts will be of home.

I am going to write to Mr. Bristow's sister who lives in Somerset, and if she invites me to visit her I will do so sometime when I get a pass. We have been having some trouble with lights lately. The electric plant in Camp here is in some disorder, so the electric lights in our huts are not working, and we have been using candles. That's why I am writing in the Y.M.C.A. Well, I will close now I wish Gústa many happy returns of her birthday. Tell her that I wish you all a very happy Christmas and a very Happy New Year.

Kiss Dad and the children for me. Give my best regards to old Maggie and all the friends. If any of my friends wish to write to me by all means give them my address. I would welcome a letter from any of them. Goodbye Dear Mother and God Bless you.

Your loving son
Archie.

Archie seemed to be settling into life at Crowborough. He was taking his machine gun training, and was a little less lonesome, although he still treasured the letters from home. Archie mentions Lieutenant Jónasson. Jónasson was originally a captain in the 108th battalion but his rank was reduced when the company went overseas.

CROWBOROUGH, SUSSEX
NOV. 20, 1916

Dear Mother,

...We had to look after some rich woman's estate about three miles from here. We were to see that no soldiers damaged her property. Some soldiers broke a tree on her place, or something like that, and now they send a patrol down there to look after the place.

We were there from five o'clock till eleven o'clock last night. We had to stay there, out in the rain, and it was midnight before I got to bed. We had to get up at six o'clock this morning, and fall in at seven o'clock to go to the ranges. We were at the ranges all day, and we will be shooting there every day this week. We have to walk about three miles to the ranges with an overcoat on, and carrying our pack and a rifle.

I was nearly all in when I got there because the road is all up and down-hill, especially after staying up so late. I'll very soon harden to it though. I wasn't the only one who was tired either.

I got a letter from Frank today, and he did not have much to say. He said he was going to London soon to see Frank Dalgleish, who is an old friend of his. Dalgleish got a job in London in the Military Pay Office.

I am going to write home as often as I can, and I want you to write often too, and also the girls. I know you are longing for letters from me and believe me, I like to get a few letters myself. Every time I receive a letter, there is a look of satisfaction and gladness on my face. You ought to see how eagerly the boys crowd around the corporal who brings the mail around. When he comes in, the boys make a dash for him.

We had a sign of winter the other day. It actually snowed here on Saturday and Sunday (yesterday), but there is no trace of snow now. It soon melted away, leaving mud puddles everywhere. We had to march through a lot of slush today.

I heard that Lieut. Jónasson received a letter from Lieut. Hallgrimur Jónsson, and Jónsson told Jónasson that he has been awarded the Military Cross for some daring night raid he had made on the Germans. I suppose you knew that he was at the front.

Well, I must quit now. Best regards to all the friends. Love to all the folks and relatives. Kiss all the children and Dad for me. God Bless you Mother.

Your Loving Son,
Archie.

A few weeks later, Archie received a letter from his cousin, Mundi, who was still stationed at South Seaford. Mundi always wrote in Icelandic, which explains the somewhat stilted phrasing. Mundi was confined to Camp due to a measles outbreak.

Mundi refers to drinking coffee with a sugar lump or, as he writes in Icelandic, *kaffi og mola*. The coffee is sipped through a sugar lump held between one's front teeth. The practice is called *molasopi*.

SOUTH SEAFORD
DEC. 5, 1916
Dear Cousin, all hail,
I am writing you a few lines, to let you know that I am alive and feeling toler-
able, except we cannot leave the Camp and are uncertain that we will be free
before Christmas—and we take it quietly and with patience, as with so many
other things. But if we get leave, and if it's at about the same time as you, then
we should get together.

I have got four letters from Canada and a big box with odds and ends of
good things. I wish that you could be here. Then I could give you coffee and a
sugar lump. I am expecting $15.00 soon from my mother, so I will have enough
money for awhile.

One letter I got was from Sigga from Kjeldulandi. She got my address
from your sister Margrjét. I have been shooting this week and doing pretty
good, so I believe I will be one of those that they will be sending to France soon.

Well, I think I must stop this nonsense this time and say good bye, from
your cousin,

Á. Einarson.

Archie's next communication was another serial letter. In this first section, he reports on his recent trip to London. Although he had a wonderful time seeing the sights, he was obviously still a typical young man with a young man's impatience.

Archie mentions walking along Rotten Row. Rotten Row is a broad track that runs along the south side of Hyde Park between Hyde Park Corner and Serpentine Road. Established at the end of the 17th century by King William III, it was originally called Route de Roi which was corrupted to become Rotten Row. It was a fashionable place for the upper classes to see and be seen.

DEC. 13TH 1916
CROWBOROUGH SUSSEX

Dear Mother,

I don't remember how long ago it is since I wrote home last. It must be quite a while. I am beginning now to make out a list of the letters I write and the date of writing so that I will know about when it is time to write again. I received a letter from Dad and one from Guðrun, one from Stjana, and and one from Lolla Freemanson.

I went to London on Dec. 2nd on a weekend pass, and had a fairly good time. Forrest Jardine is my bed mate here, and he is a pretty good scout. Harry Palmason and Swanie [Sveinn] Johnson and Jardine and I all went to London that weekend. Harry and Swanie were together, and Jardine and I were together. I did not see much of Harry and Swanie in London.

Jardine and I went all over the principal port of the city in a Y.M.C.A. automobile, and the ride did not cost us anything. We went into the St. Paul's Cathedral, and it was grand. This was Sunday morning and there was a Divine service on. The music was excellent. We only stayed in there about 5 minutes.

We went past the King's palace. There was quite a crowd of people at the gate waiting to see if the King was going for a drive. The King's carriage was at the door, so we stopped to see if the King was going to appear, but no such luck. A lady dressed in black got into the carriage in a hurry, and off they went.

Then we went along Rotten Row. It is a long promenade or driveway. That's where London society goes out riding on Sunday for exercise. A crowd of these big bugs were riding up and down.

Then we went by the Serpentine, which is a long artificial waterway, which is long and rather crooked. That's why it gets the name "Serpentine". We also went past the Post Office, the War Office and the Houses of Parliament (House of Lords and House of Commons).

We went along Piccadilly and Leicester Square. We also went past the tower where the Bow Bells were. They are the bells that used to ring for Dick Whittington in olden days.

Well, Dear Mother, it is getting late, and I must soon be making my bed and be going to bed, so I will say Good Night and will continue this letter to-morrow. Good night.

Your son,
Archie

As he mentioned in this letter to his mother, Archie prepared a list of people he planned to write. He wrote the list on the back of a slip of paper which bore the names and addresses of several young ladies he met while on leave in London, likely at a mixer of some sort.

Archie seemed to have had a way with the ladies. He had seven sisters, so it is not surprising that he was quite comfortable talking to girls. Doris Bass, who apparently was also at the mixer, was on the list of persons that Archie intended to write. We will hear more about Doris later.

On December 14th, Archie continued the letter to his mother by bringing her up to date on recent events. He and virtually all of his friends were quarantined due to an outbreak of measles. We see Archie's wry sense of humour when he tells Elísabet that "the measles are getting popular."

THURSDAY, DECEMBER 14TH, EVENING.
I have just had supper, so I will start on this letter once more. I did not tell you last night that we were in quarantine. Two boys in our section took sick with the measles a little over a week ago and were sent to the hospital. We

were quarantined on Dec. 6th, and the quarantine is to last sixteen days from that date if no more cases break out. If everything goes well, we will be out just before Xmas, and might possibly get leave at Xmas.

We are supposed to get six days leave. I intend to spend about one or two days in London, and the remainder of my leave with Mrs. Tyler of Highbridge (Mr. Bristow's sister). I got a letter from her today, and she was asking me when I would get my leave. She said that she is going to book some seats at the Bristol Pantomime Theatre when I go to see her.

I have written several letters to her, and she answers them promptly. She writes me very nice letters. I think that I'll send you one of the letters that she wrote me. I got a letter from Mundi lately, and he has been quarantined like myself. He has been to the ranges, though, and he says he did pretty good shooting, and expects to be sent to the front with the first draft from the 108th. At least he thought it likely.

But then Swanie got a letter the other night from Laugi Hjorleifson, and he thought that they would be quarantined quite a while longer. I suppose some more measles have broken out at their Camp. I got a letter from Frank the other night, and he has been quarantined for some time. So you see, the measles are getting popular.

Frank is attached to the Signal Base at Seaford. I suppose that Aunt Nina [Frank Polson's mother] has already told you this. He says that he is feeling fine, and having an easy time. The first days that we were in quarantine, we had an easy time. Now we get physical exercise, route marches and squad drill every day. We would sooner have an easy, lazy time, but perhaps it is just as well that we get plenty of exercise. At least it helps to keep us in shape and condition.

I have not received a parcel from home yet, but I guess it must be on its way. I am sure I will get it in a few days. Some of the other boys of the section have been getting parcels from home, and they have always treated the boys of the section.

Jardine got a parcel the other night, and he only had one piece of the cake himself. I guess that it will be the same when I get a parcel. The mailman has just come around, and I stopped writing to read them. I got five letters, one from you and Margaret dated Nov. 23rd, one from Josie, one from

Bonnie, one from Mabel Hermanson from Selkirk and one from her sister Lolla Hermanson.

You were asking me whether I received the money that was sent to me. I got the money order alright and the two dollars from Wyatt, and the dollar which was from the Old Women's subscription. But then you mention another dollar sent later, which I have not received. I might get it yet, though. Every cent I get from home has helped quite a bit.

We have not been paid all that has been coming to us since we came to England. They have been taking five dollars per month off our pay, or rather holding it back. I don't exactly know why. I think that they are keeping back five dollars per month until we have fifteen dollars to our credit. That is what we have been told. It is taken in case we get a long leave when we get back from the front. Some say that it is in case that we get killed at the front, and that the government would pay the held-back amount to our relatives.

Some say that they won't pay the assigned pay after we are dead, and they will keep the fifteen dollars so that they won't be out of pocket. This may not be true, but then we have never heard any responsible information why this is held back. We have asked our lieutenant and sergeants, but they claim they don't know. I guess we will get along better after New Year as this is the third month we have been here, and by the end of the month they will have their fifteen dollars in their hands.

We will likely get more pay after that. We have only been getting about £2 per month on the average. I have got along fairly well on that, together with the money I received from home. I don't know whether you have sent any lately, but any way I think I'll get along alright after this.

It is when I get a pass that I need money most. And it is when on pass that we get the only amusement or good times. We can't have any fun in Camp. The only entertainment we have here is a concert in the Y.M.C.A. or in the recreation hall of the depot, but they are not up to much. We could go to the town of Crowborough, but there is nothing worthwhile going to as the town is about two miles from Camp.

I am sure that I will have a good time when I go to see Mrs. Tyler. I think we will start on the machine gun course about New Years. That course will take us at least six weeks so I don't think I will be sent to the front till late in February unless they need the men extra urgently. If they need the men extra bad, they might hurry us through the course and make the course shorter, but I hardly think it probable. Of course, you never can tell.

I would advise you to address all parcels to Army Post Office, London but it is alright to address all letters to G.M.G.D. Crowborough. I know that they forward letters to soldiers who have gone to the front. Of course, when I leave for France, I will let you know how to address the letters differently, if it is advisable.

One of the boys of the section got a parcel from home two days ago, and it left Winnipeg about October 26th. Another lad got a parcel today, and it was mailed about the end of October. So you see the parcels are a long time coming, and I might have to wait about two weeks before I get mine. I wish you would send me ten dollars when you get this letter. If you send it to me shortly after you get this letter, the money ought to reach me about the first of February. If you find it hard to raise the money so soon, then wait till you can send it. As long as I get it before the 15th of February I will be happy.

I might possibly need the money to get some things before I go to the trenches. I know that I am expecting, or rather asking pretty much of you for I know you need all the money you get. If I could get this money from you, I would be pretty sure to be on the safe side. But regarding the fifteen dollars that is held back on us, that is taken off our pay and not the money I signed over to you. I don't think the government will take it off your money as well as mine, but if they do you will know that they have no business to do it.

But it is not for us soldiers to dictate what the Canadian government must do or must not do. We have got to do what we are told. Some of the boys have said that they can't refuse to give us six days leave at Christmas but I have found out that the authorities don't ask us what we are entitled to or what we are not entitled to. They have us where they want us and, and as they say, ours is not to reason why, ours is but to do or die. I am not grumbling, but I think there might be better systems in some places.

Well, it is getting late in the evening, so I will leave off for the present. I will continue tomorrow night.

Good night dear mother,
Your son, Archie.

P.S. *Will get a bunch of parcels when they start coming.*

Archie finished his letter on the following evening.

FRIDAY DEC. 15TH EVENING.

I'll be getting quite a few things by the look of things. I'll get a parcel from home and the tobacco from Dad and a parcel from Bonnie, one from Lolla Freemanson, one from Stjana and one from the Good Templars [a fraternal organization devoted to temperance that was active in the Icelandic community].

The mailman has just been here and I got a letter from Frank. He says he is in good health, but still in quarantine. His bedmate took sick with the measles, but Frank did not get a touch of it. He expected to be out of quarantine by Xmas. I got a letter from Mundi today and he is still in quarantine. He said he expected that they would be in quarantine about two weeks longer, and after that they expect to be sent to France. He says he will be glad to get out of that damnable Camp.

The Canadians don't get the best Camps. For instance, the Camp I am in, is a muddy, sloppy Camp. We can't step outside the door without getting all muddy. But the country surrounding the Camp is very pretty, although we don't have much chance to see it. We haven't got much spare time, and even then most of the area is out of bounds to us. We have been able to see a little of it lately when we go on our route marches. The other day we went past an old mill, which was run by water but which is out of use now. There are streams and ponds everywhere. Today, we saw a little artificial waterfall that was very pretty.

The meals we get now are not too bad. They were not any too good when we first came, but we kept on kicking so they are a little better now. Mundi said that he will be glad when we get the tobacco from Dad. We had a little snow this morning, but it was so little that it did not even cover the ground, and it disappeared a few hours afterward, leaving the roads sloppy. We hardly realize that this is the winter season. The weather is so mild that we think it is fall. We haven't had much rain lately. When we go out for physical exercise, we have no cap on, no mitts, no overcoat or tunic, but we wear our sweaters.

We haven't had a sunshiny day for a long time. The days have been dull, and sometimes foggy. I have a bunch of letters to answer and that will keep me busy for a while.

Be sure and give my best regards to all the friends, and tell them I am getting along fine and will soon mow the Germans down with a machine gun. I am getting sick of England—at least where I am now—and I don't think that I'll be sorry when I leave for the front.

If we got well paid and got week end passes more often, it would not be so bad. Returned soldiers get more money, and longer leave than we do. Well, I must close now and answer some of the other letters, and besides I can't think of anything more to write.

So Good Bye, your loving son
Archie Polson 721948
"A" Company
Canadian M.G. Depot
Crowborough Sussex

P.S. Kiss Dad and the children for me.

Archie wrote to his father two days after he finished his letter to his mother.

SUNDAY EVENING
DEC. 17TH 1916
CROWBOROUGH, SUSSEX
Dear Dad,
Many thanks for your letter received several days ago. I have been pretty busy writing letters as I have received quite a bunch this last week. I received a letter from Mundi. He is in quarantine, and expects to remain in until after New Year. Afterwards, he expects that they will be sent to France shortly. He said he will be glad when the tobacco which you are sending arrives.

Frank is in quarantine, and so am I. I expect we will be out by Christmas. Frank expects to get out of it about that time. I don't know when I will get my Christmas leave. I might not get it till New Years. I am going to Somerset to see Mrs Tyler. She is Mr. Bristow's sister.

I did a lot of washing today. I washed two towels, about six pair of socks, a suit of underwear, about five handkerchiefs and a fatigue shirt. And now I am writing while the washing dries. We have not been able to send away any laundry since we were quarantined. My writing is kind of shaky as I have just been dancing a Highland fling to the music of a mouth organ.

I have had a bath twice since we were quarantined, but did not have any clean underwear to put on. At least, I am going to have clean clothes when I go on pass. If you were here, you would not think it was winter time. We have had a little frost in the mornings, like we have down home in the mornings of early October. The worst of it is that the weather is seldom clear. It is often foggy. We have had enough to do though we are quarantined. We have been going on route marches and doing physical exercise every day.

It is nearly impossible to get Canadian tobacco here. I haven't seen any Old Chum tobacco around except with some of the boys who had it sent from home. McDonalds Chewing tobacco costs nine pence here, that is, eighteen cents.

The last time I was in London, I went for an automobile ride through London. I wrote to mother about it. No doubt you have seen the letter. I think it is needless to write it over again. I haven't had many newspapers from home. I would like to get both [the] Free Press and [the] Icelandic papers. I got a letter from Stjana a few days ago, and she said Gimli was dead and said that she missed you in the store. [S & T had sent Ágúst to work at their Riverton store]. We were taking bomb throwing here before we were quarantined, and I told Stjana that I would like to scatter a few bombs in Gimli to stir things up a bit.

When you write next, tell me all about the business and how the fishermen are getting on. I guess you will be busy when you receive this. How is Thorður getting along with his fishing? How would you like to have me working in the store with you? You would not have to break me in very much.

By the look of things I don't think I will go to France until about the middle of February. I was surprised to hear that Fúsi Bergman was married. I remember how he used to talk against enlisting. We boys are always kicking, but still we would not miss it for anything. I am sure if we were civilians again, we would enlist again. If I ever get back to Canada, I will have a lot of things to talk about.

Give my love to Guðrun, Snyder and Jóhanna—and all the folks at home. Give my best regards to my Thorvaldson cousins and to all the friends. Write as often as you can.

Merry Xmas and Happy New Year to all the folks.

Your loving son
Archie.

Archie received another letter written in Icelandic from his cousin, Mundi Einarson. It appears that, despite its date, the letter is the one to which Archie referred in the third sentence of his December 17 letter to his father.

SOUTH SEAFORD
DEC. 18, 1916
Dear Cousin, all hail,
I am going to write you a few lines as I am sending you ten shillings. No news have I to tell you, but I am feeling all right for the most part, except we get rather little food and we are still locked [up] in [Camp], and most likely will be for another two weeks. They tell us that then we will be shipped out. That will be good because I have had enough of my stay here.

I got your letter last night. I am looking forward to receiving the tobacco that you are sending to us and hope we will get it. You will let me know when you get this.

Here is good bye from your friend and cousin,
Einarson

Archie wrote to Elísabet early in the New Year, and tells her about Christmas and New Year's in Camp. He also reports on the state of health of other Gimli soldiers, and he makes a rather ominous comment about how he is safe while he is in England, and it will take "real steel bullets or shrapnel or something like that" to kill him.

CROWBOROUGH
CAN. M.G. DEPOT
SUSSEX
JAN 2ND 1917
Dear Mother,

I received your registered letter on Xmas day with ten dollars enclosed, and also the large box from you all. Isn't it a coincidence that I should get it on Xmas Day? We had a swell dinner on Xmas Day. One of the huts was fixed up and decorated, and tables and benches were put in there for the occasion. I was at dinner when my Xmas box came and one of the boys came in and said that there was a young coffin waiting for me in the hut. He meant the Xmas box.

For Xmas dinner, we had goose and peas and dressing, and plum pudding galore. We had fruit and nuts, and everybody came away with a full stomach. We had a fine time. Some of the officers came in and gave us a speech. You see, all of "A" company ate together. Each company had a hut fixed up for Xmas dinner. We had New Year's dinner last night at five o'clock. It was a good meal. We had roast beef for dinner.

After dinner I went to a dance in Crowborough, and came home at 11:30. The dance was pretty good, but many of the dances are different from what I am used to. They dance the Lancers, the Quadrille, the Veleta, Barn Dance and Boston Two-Step. Of course, I can dance the Waltz and Two-Step and One-Step and Fox Trot with them, but I have not tried the Lancers or the Veleta. I don't think I'll go down there very often as I lose too much sleep.

I don't know when I will go to France. It might be six or eight weeks before I go. I have heard rumors that we might go sooner than that, and finish our training in France, but I don't know if there is any truth in it.

I haven't been able to get my six-day Xmas pass yet, and don't know whether I will ever get it. I might get a weekend pass to London soon, but I can't go to see Mrs. Tyler on a weekend pass. However, we are entitled to a four day pass before we go to the front. That four day pass is called the "Kings Leave."

We have been having fairly good weather lately. It has hardly rained at all, and no snow and very little frost. Well, Dear Mother, I have had good health right along, and that is something to be thankful for. So don't worry about me, they can't kill me here in England. It takes real steel bullets or shrapnel or something like that to kill me.

Give my love to all the friends. I wish you all a Joyous New Year.

With love and Kisses from your loving son
Archie

In the next two letters, Archie tells of his last leave and his efforts to visit his cousins, Frank and Mundi, before departing for France. True to form, he tries to reassure his mother that he is willing to accept his fate, whatever that may be.

SUNDAY
CROWBOROUGH SUSSEX
FEB. 4TH 1917
Dear Mother,
When I wrote to you last I was at Mrs. Tyler's. I went to visit her when I was on my last leave. I got my leave with the rest of the boys last Monday (a week ago tomorrow). I intended to go and see Frank and Mundi but could not go to Shorncliffe [a Canadian Army Camp located in Kent] where they are now as my pass was not made out to that place, so I needed a special voucher.

We got our railway tickets free, and when I got my ticket I told them that I wanted to go to Shorncliffe, as well as to Highbridge. They told me all I had to do was to show my free warrant ticket at the station in London, and I could rebook to Shorncliffe. When I got to London I couldn't get a ticket to Shorncliffe, because I didn't have a voucher. So I just stayed in London until my pass was up and I had to go back to Camp.

We have been busy all day today getting ready to go to France on draft [a military expression meaning to be shipped to a war zone]. We expected to go tomorrow but we might not go till the day after. But we will be going to France in a few days. It is getting late in the evening and I must go to bed. I will write again tomorrow if I have time. I received the money order last night which you sent me.

Good night Dear Mother,
Your loving son, Archie.

P.S. I will write as often as I can and will let you know my address in France as soon as I get there. I am sending you a booklet with pictures of Crowborough.

CROWBOROUGH
FEB. 6TH 1917
Dear Mother,

I am going on draft tomorrow morning with the rest of our section. We will have to get up at 3 o'clock tomorrow morning and will start early I expect. I will let you know my new address when I get to France. It is 10 P.M. now and I must make this letter short. I am in good health and am looking forward to seeing France, whatever it may have in store for me.

Give my love to all. Be brave, Dear Mother. The Lord will spare me for you if He deems it advisable for all concerned. I will write as often as possible.

With love and kisses,
Your ever loving son,
Archie.

P.S. Will you please show the scenery postcards I sent you to Stjana Orr? Show them to her. I am sure she would like to see them.

CHAPTER FIVE

IN THE TRENCHES

ARCHIE SET OUT FOR FRANCE ON FEBRUARY 7, and wrote to his mother on February 14, although only part of the letter survives. Judging from his touching and revealing comments about his impending departure for the Front, he must have had a sense of what he was about to experience. The truth is that he was scared. He missed all aspects of his life at home, a fact borne out by his intention to write to his former employer.

[…] the local news and gossip. There are so many people I want to write to, but I haven't got time to write to them all. I nearly always start by writing to you and very often I have not done more than to write to you. When I have written a long letter to you, I have not felt like writing any more at a time. Give all my love to all our old friends and relatives and tell them I'm doing fine. Kiss Dad and all the children for me. Don't ever worry about me as I am getting along fine. The army will look after me. Just keep on praying for me, as you have always done. I am prepared to die any time that the Lord wills it. I firmly believe it will be heaven for me when I die. I don't think anybody can say that I haven't been a pretty good boy these twenty-one years of my life. Well, goodbye Dear Mother, God bless you all, and keep in best of health and spirits. Heaps of love and a thousand kisses from your loving son,

Archie Polson.

P.S. The old song "Just before the Battle, Mother" has entered my thoughts, and it seems to bring tender thoughts of the dear ones at home. If anyone asks how I'm getting on, tell them that I'm in France and will soon be on the firing line. Send me Jóhannes Sigurdson's address. I am thinking of writing to him when

I have time, just for old times' sake. I saw Lieut. Jónasson in Crowborough. He was taking [an] Officer's Course. He looked fine. He is fatter than I have ever seen him before. I have not written to Bonnie or Josie for a long time but you can tell them I will do so as soon as I find time.
My address is:

> *721948 Pte. A. J. Polson*
> *Canadian M. G. Pool*
> *Care – Anzac A.P.O.*
> *Section 18*
> *France*

Let Bonnie and Josie and Stjana Orr know about my new address.

"Just before the Battle, Mother" is an American song often sung during Victoria Day celebrations in Canada in the nineteenth and early twentieth century. Here is the first verse and chorus:

> Just before the battle, mother,
> I am thinking most of you,
> While upon the field we're watching
> With the enemy in view.
> Comrades brave are 'round me lying,
> Filled with thoughts of home and God
> For well they know that on the morrow,
> Some will sleep beneath the sod.
> CHORUS:
> Farewell, mother, you may never
> Press me to your heart again,
> But, oh, you'll not forget me, mother,
> If I'm numbered with the slain.

Archie was right to be worried about what the future held for him. Much has been written about the life of a soldier fighting on the Western Front, especially by British writers. Dr. Paul Mulvey, a teacher at the London School of Economics, wrote about trench life in a scholarly essay delivered as a lecture:

Nonetheless, the trenches were very dangerous, for as well as the obvious dangers during an attack, the closeness of the front lines meant constant exposure to sniping, shelling, gas attacks or trench raids [...] Death and injury came in a number of ways—via machine guns, rifles, grenades, gas, mines, mortars, flame-throwers and shells—though most commonly via bullets (about 40% of casualties) or shells (50+%). Bullets couldn't be heard until they had gone past. There was often little bleeding from the wound they caused, just a bluish aperture as the bullet cauterised as it went. Ricochets and short-range bullets did much more obvious damage. The wounds of such bullets (15 square inch gapes) could break the nerve of onlookers. While men with ½ their heads shot off might take an hour or two to die—and be conscious all the time.

Shells injured and killed in a number of ways—a man might entirely disappear—vaporised. He might be blown to pieces. Or he might appear entirely uninjured, except that the shock-wave had ruptured his kidneys and spleen, so killing him. And if only wounded by fragments of the shell, the wound, in those pre-antibiotic days, would almost inevitably go septic because of the dirt blown into it along with the flying metal.

As if being shot and shelled were not bad enough, the front line trenches themselves offered a constant reminder of death. The men were living in a charnel house of decomposing flesh, rats and flies, and many veterans went to their graves haunted by the images of corpses. The newly dead, or those in life-like positions, had the worst effect, and tended to undermine morale, no matter how tough or experienced the observer.

The unburied dead, of course, encouraged vermin, as did the inability of the front line men to keep themselves clean—there were no baths or showers in the trenches—with lice and fleas to add to the discomforts of rats and flies. Under such circumstances, parasitic illnesses were common, such as trench fever—spread by lice excreta—and scabies—caused by mites.[34]

In less scholarly but more vivid terms, popular historical writer Terry Breverton has also written on the subject:

The front line troops lived with rotting corpses. No man's land in the Ypres Salient at any one time had 10,000 dismembered, fetid corpses rotting on the ground, thus the shrine for the Unknown Soldier was placed there. When shellfire hit these decomposing bodies, parts would be flung into the trenches, hitting the occupants. Often, during a battle, bombardment would destroy the trenches and they would have to be re-dug. It was common practice during combat to hastily bury dozens of bodies in shell holes. When trenches were re-dug, they would regularly have to dig through these mass graves, which involved hacking off green maggot-ridden limbs. Huge rats fed on the corpses, growing so large and fearless that they often killed badly wounded soldiers. A French soldier wrote of Germans, killed by machine guns, who lay in front of his trench for over a month: "lined up as if on manoeuvre. The rain falls on them inexorably and bullets shatter their bleached bones. One evening on patrol, we saw enormous rats fleeing from under their faded coats. They were fat with animal meat. A friend of mine, his heart pounding, crawled toward a dead man with a grimacing face, no flesh, skull bare, eyes eaten. Out of his gaping mouth a foul animal jumped."[35]

Elísabet received Archie's letters of February 3 and February 5, but had not received his letter of February 14 when she wrote to him on February 25. She sends him a long, newsy letter in Icelandic, updating him on the events at home. Elísabet has heard Archie's girlfriend, Stjana Orr, is seeing a young man named Pálmi Lárusson. Elísabet buries the revelation in the narrative, apparently to lessen the blow. Stjana would later marry Pálmi.

Elísabet refers to a place called Stjarna. *Stjarna* is Icelandic for star. No record of Stjarna has been found. It was likely a settlement that has been long abandoned.

GIMLI MAN.
FEB. 25 1917
My dearest Archie,
And now you are in France, my dear boy.

I trust God to keep His blessed hand over you and us all, and help us to be together again, if that is His will. On Friday, I got the last two letters that you wrote in England.

Last night Wyatt went north to Riverton to spend time with dad, and I did send your letters with him. I know he wants to get them right away. One thing I know for sure, and it is even clearer to me now, how much he cares for you, more than what he showed when you were here at home. But your mother is always the same. She is not afraid to let her children know how much she loves them and trusts them.

Today Florence is nineteen years old. She is still in Winnipeg and expects that she will be there for another week. It is hard for me to lose her for so long, because now I have to do all my work alone and also look after the children. But it will work out somehow.

Now Lilly Olsen has had a son, so Gestur has become a father. On Thursday evening Marsibil, the wife of Jonathan, died and the funeral will be this coming Tuesday.

The Minister Mr. Olson is good from his operation, but he is now feeling sick in his head. He got that after he got better. He went to Dr. Jón Stefansson for advice, but he is home now.

I still have not got the pictures you sent me, but I will show Stjana them when I get them. Whether she will look at them, I can´t tell you. People say that all her eyes are on young Pálmi Lárusson. He has enough money now, but I don´t know about that or other things.

Auntie Nína is entertaining Florence tonight, by inviting a few girls home. That will be Lolla Freemanson and the girls who are staying with her. Lóa Sigmundsson has asked for your address. She said she is going to scold you for forgetting your old friends.

Mrs Jóhanna Sólmundsson has issued a summons against Jóhann. She wants the children and fifty dollars per month. She says that there is another woman, but I don't know if that's true.

Gústa still works for Mr. McLeod, but tomorrow Margrjét will be there because Mr. L. is going to Selkirk to see his wife.

Not much is happening with The Ladies Aid this winter. I don´t have time to meet with them but nobody is doing their duty, so I must do something soon, This [sic] laziness won't do. My Bonnie is doing well, and I have heard *that her patients like her very much. All the Gimli people ask about you. They have not forgotten you.*

Thórður has started work at Sigurðsson, so the store is doing better than before. I have heard that Pálmi has taking the place of L. Johnson in the office in Stjarna. Helgi Benson is back to the north lake and moved into the late Mrs. Lilly Thorarinson's house

I can't remember much more to tell you. I would like it if I could get a picture of yourself in the near future. Everybody sends you greetings my dear.

God be with you my loving son from your loving mother,
E. Th. Polson

Ever the considerate son, the last thing Archie would have wanted would be to reveal the predicament in which he now found himself. So in his first letter from the Front, he makes light of it all, even his first close brush with death. Archie is still broke, more broke than before, and asking for cigarettes and treats.

MAR. 3 1917
SOMEWHERE IN FRANCE
Dear Mother,
At last I am in the trenches. I am right in the front line trench and I find it interesting at times and sometimes it gets a little exciting (and then some). There were only four of our old M.G. Section came to this part of the country. There are two Icelanders besides myself, but I only see them once in a while.

A sniper nearly got me the other day but as luck would have it he missed me by a couple of feet. Since then, I have kept my head down nearer the ground. If you saw me sometimes you would say I looked like old Friman (you know, Ben Frimanson's father) only I walk a little more stooped than he does. That is to say, I do sometimes but not always. I have been in good health since I came out here. That is one consolation.

I have not received any mail since I came to France but I guess I will soon get some, now that I have settled down to business.

I would like you to send me some cake and tarts and some homemade toffee and nut bars and chocolate bars, or anything that's good to eat in the line of sweets. I would like also a few packages of Players cigarettes, and about two packages of Old Chum tobacco and a packet of cigarette papers. I would also like you to send me a pair of socks, but not very heavy socks as the weather is getting a good deal warmer.

You told me in some of your letters that I should let you know if I wanted anything. Well, Mother dear, how do you like this big order to start with?

If you could spare me five dollars, it would help me a great deal. We don't get as much money here as we did in England. I got paid once since I arrived in France, but when I came into the trenches I was broke. I didn't have a cent. We get four packages of cigarettes issued to us each week and that has kept me partly in smokes. I don't know what I would have done for smokes if it had not been for that. But I don't like the cigarettes they give us, as well as I do Players cigarettes.

Send me a pair of woolen mitts. If you send the money, send it by Money Order on Army P.O. London. I wrote to Frank and Mundi, and to Mrs. Tyler when I was at the machine gun pool, but have not had an answer from them yet. I don't know whether Mundi or Frank are in France or England. I know that they were still in England when I came across.

You can tell all my friends that I am in the trenches and that I send them all my best regards. Give my regards to Jón. Sigurdson and family and send me their address. Tell me all about what is going on around Gimli. I will close now. Kiss Dad and the Kiddies for me.

With Heaps of love from your loving son
Archie
721948 Prt. A.J. Polson 5th Canadian M.G. Company
B.E.F. France

Elísabet had not received Archie's letter of March 3 when she wrote to him again in Icelandic on March 18. The letter is quite long, and includes much gossip. Elísabet has bad news to tell Archie. Ágúst has lost his job and the home they are renting has been sold. Once again, Elísabet buries it in the letter so as not to overly alarm Archie.

Also, a young person named Blythe is staying with the Polsons. She appears to be a member or friend of the McLeod family and apparently the McLeod house has been quarantined. Mrs. McLeod initially was not going to come to visit Blythe but then changes her mind.

Margrjét is unwell, her illness later diagnosed as an early case of "Spanish Flu", an epidemic that would eventually sweep the globe.

GIMLI MAN.
MARCH 18 1917

My dearest Archie,

My deep thanks and appreciation for your letter which I received on March 12th, although it was dated February 14th.

How I was pleased to hear that you were not on the line, as you call it. I have the feeling in my mind that I am with you every step, and now I feel that you are getting closer to the line, my dearest boy, but we must both put our trust in God, and with Him nothing is impossible. I know that with you manner, you will show that you have a mother and God who love you, and I trust you will get through it all. I can tell you about your father and siblings.

The children are all at Sunday School, and your father is up North. Blythe is sleeping upstairs. She is still here, and will be this month. Mrs. McLeod is all better but won't come down yet. [Elísabet takes a break from writing] Now the children are home and Blythe is awake. I had to quit writing because Bergthór Skarðarson and Mrs.Josephine Jóhannsson and also Mrs. McLeod came to take Blythe out. But now they are gone and I have some peace again. I gave them coffe, but now I soon have to think about supper.

Bergthór told me that old Helga is moving with her daughter Fríða in [illegible] Brook and Hannes is going with her and Tryggvi is taking Óli and taking him west to his mother.

Benidikt Freemansson was operated on at the General Hospital on Tuesday. Nobody knows what that was about but it was a very serious operation and nobody knows if he will survive

Solla got her mother, but old Freeman went to the Betel Old folks Home and the house is closed in the mean time.

But now old Jón Sæmaland's gone. He died on March 3rd at the Hospital in Selkirk but old Hlíf is in Betel. Mr. and Mrs Christie are running what we call moving pictures show on Ellice Ave. But I don't know how well it is going for them.

Siggi Kristjánsson has sold his house here for one thousand. Mr. Johnson, husband of Rúna from Skíðastaðir, bought it. I don't know what Siggi is going to do. Guðmundur Finnsson is moving his house over to Central Street, just across from where Sveinn was. He bought a lot from Eggert Sigurðsson from Selkirk.

Sveinn Björnsson has moved to Sanders store, but Mundi Pálsson is in the store where Sveinn was and operates a blacksmith's shop.

Mrs. Jósephine Jóhannsson is having her house moved over to the lot that Ingibjörg from Skipalæk owned. Sigthrúður, Sam's mother, is going to move hers south of Sveinn Geirholm. Lilly Olson is all better now and I have heard that her son is to be named Norman.

Blessed Frank Polson wrote to me to let me know of you, and to tell me that you are getting along better than he is. He is only in C company. I am sure he is still the good boy that he always was.

Then now is best that I now tell you the home news. The first is that Joe [Jóhannes] Sigurdson and Svein [Thorvaldson] have given your father notice that they won't be needing him after this month, and your father has to find another work. I want to go to [illegible] but your father would rather not, because Pete Tergesen [H.P. Tergesen's son] offered him work. Your dad only asked for wages of $65 per month, but he will get a raise if Tergesen can see fit.

I have heard through the grapevines that our house has been sold, and we must move. We have not been told anything, but it will all come out in its time. I am not uneasy, because I try to trust the Good Lord.

Tergesen is remodeling the whole store, and Snyder is to paint the inside and make an ice cream parlour and other things that I don't know about. I only have this from others. [Elísabet takes another break from writing.] Again I had to stop, because Mrs McLeod came in with Blythe and stayed for supper, then I had to go out to the barn. Everything has to be done on time. Wyatt had a mishap. One of his sheep had two lambs, but they were both dead when he came out in the morning. It happened on the 4th. The others have not delivered yet. Pat [apparently a pet dog] is very much in favourite here. We thought it better to have him because he is so good to Blythe. He does nothing even though she is playing with him.

Snæbjörn will be moving from Riverton the end of this month and I believe Núni will come here with little Jóhanna while Snæbjörn decides what his plan will be. He has so many ideas in his head. Where it stops is hard to say. Don't you think it will be full house if Josie, Leona [Josie's sister-in-law] and Jóhanna and Núni will all be here? Old Maggie is again asking me to take her back. She has so often asked me, but I am trying to stall it as long as I can.

Florence is back home and is working at McLeods [Bakery]. She starts working at 2 p.m. and stays until after train time. She gets 50 cents per day. She helps me before noon. Margrjét is not doing well going to school. The doctor is looking at her tomorrow, to see if she is well enough to continue, but Konráð goes to school and Wyatt and Gústa go to the the minister [for confirmation instruction]. He is now well again.

Karin is working at the dray store again. Ósk is no longer there.

Gumbi and Hannes are opening the Restaurant again. They had it after the Samuel's left.

Old Ingibjörg the daughter of Sigurður has been very ill this winter. Sister has been at the same place and everyone is feeling hopefull. Her children have been sick. Einar Westmann has moved to Selkirk. They left yesterday and Jón the white isalso moving there.

I went this week to see the Bristows and Mrs. Bristow and she is feeling fine and Bristow was good, and he had good luck at the lake over the winter.

Johnie Goodman is working in Morris. He had the measles this winter. Old Jón and Halldóra are with the same. Maggie Goodman is in Selkirk. She has been ill but is little better now. She has been bedridden for seven weeks. Her Grandmother is now dead. She was just shy of 100 years when she died.

I think I have now written everything I can about the people I can think of. Most people are feeling well, except all else is well except the Good Templar Organization which I am told is attended by few.

My dear child, how I cherish your last letter. It was so thoughtful, and I can see that you are the same loving boy that you always were. I sent the letter *right away to your father [in Riverton], and then it goes to Bonnie and she promised that she will read it to your grandmother. I can't remember anything more to tell you this time. Everybody sends their greetings. May God Almighty be with you always.*

Your loving mother that I am.
E. Th. Polson

Archie's younger brother, Wyatt, was only thirteen years of age in 1916 but the boys had a strong filial bond. Wyatt idolized his big brother, the brave soldier. In his first letter to Wyatt from the Front, Archie once again chooses not to reveal the reality of his life in the trenches. We also see Archie's impish sense of humour again when he says that he would feel much more like writing if Wyatt would send him some nut bars and chocolate. Particularly telling is the invocation at the top of the first page of the letter.

Be good to Mother and Dad and do your work with a will.

SOMEWHERE IN THE TRENCHES FRANCE
MAR. 11TH 1917
Dear Wyatt,
I received your very welcome letter last night, and was very pleased to get it. It sure was a nice long newsy letter.

It was very interesting to hear about the dog race and those newspaper clippings were interesting. I would like to hear more about the dog race. I would like to know who won it. I got a letter from Bonnie last night, and she said that it was not an Icelander who won it.

Doddi Thordarson must have been silly to think that he had any chance of winning. I guess he got his name put in the paper and that might have given him some satisfaction. Has he got good dogs? Did he use his own dogs in the race?

I have been in good health since I came into the trenches. I received a letter from Frank the other night. He is still in England and is in good health. He sees Mundi quite often. I have not heard from Mundi for a long time.

I received a letter from Josie last night. She tells me that you folks back in Manitoba have been having a lot of snow. The weather out here is getting fairly warm now, and I expect it will be getting warmer every day, which, of course, stands to reason.

I am writing this in a trench, and I can hear the shells bursting around me. They are not coming very close, for, if that were the case, I would mighty soon go down into our dugout. But I expect there will be a time when I will have to stay outside and face the music.

Well little brother, a fellow does not feel like writing very much news out here. Then there are some things which you might find interesting to read, which I am not allowed to write about.

I have seen some aeroplane fights since I came here. One day, I saw one of our aeroplanes bring down a German aeroplane. It was quite an interesting sight to see. If you would send me some chocolate and a couple of packages of Players Cigarettes I might feel more inclined to write. It might put me in a writing mood. Nut bars and plain chocolate taste pretty good out here.

I can understand that you have plenty of work to do when you have to haul water for the house, and also for the cow besides all the other chores. I remember the time when I found it hard work. But then, I went through the same work when I was your age (if I remember right) and I expect that you should be able to stand it, (seeing that you are a chip off the same block). I hope you will write me another long letter like the last one and tell me the news from the old town.

Mundi's address is:

721913 Pte. A. Einarson

No. 2 Company

14th Canadian Reserve Bn

Dibgate Camp

Shorncliffe England

I will now close this scrawl. Kiss Mother and Dad, and Konnie and all the sisters for me. Give my regards to all the friends, with love and good wishes from your big brother.

7221948 Pte. A.J. Polson

5th Canadian M.G. Company

A letter from Wyatt was sent after Archie was wounded, but before the family had been notified. Wyatt gives a nice sense of the family's bucolic life. He brings Archie up to date on the local gossip, including a report on Doddi Thordarson's dog race that Archie asked about in his last letter. Wyatt mentions that Doddi lost to a "half-breed". The term "half-breed" is now considered to be a derogative expression. In Archie's day, the word merely described a person of mixed Scottish and First Nations ancestry, as opposed to a Métis who is a person of French and First Nations ancestry. It was not necessarily meant as—or taken as—an insult.

Wyatt mentions that "Guðrún is downtown buying a money order for Simpson's". The Robert Simpson Company—commonly known as Simpson's—was a Canadian department store founded in 1858 and conducted an active mail order business. It would later be called Simpson-Sears, and eventually Sears Canada.

APRIL 11TH, 1917,

Dear Archie,

I received your most welcome mail yesterday morning because we never got our mail night before last because Uncle [Snyder] was too late for the mail because he had no keys.

Mother and Father came home night before last. They brought me a suit of clothes and three shirts, one white, one blue, one white with black stripes. It makes me think of stars and stripes (U.S.). They have joined in with the Allies on Mother's birthday [on April 6].

My Easter present was three lambs from the old sheep. One ram and two female sheep. I had two before from the younger one, but they both died, and the reason why, I do not know that. One morning when I came out, they lay there, both solid frozen on the floor of your shed because we now have that for your sheep house. We moved it over to longside [sic] the stable, and put the sheep in it.

Uncle [Snyder] and Guðrún are here with Jóhanna. She is walking along the floor. They have come for good. Guðrún is downtown buying a money order for Simpson's. I am alone with Jóhanna and Konnie is taking care of her. Fjóla brought Blythe's go-cart over so as to take Jóhanna out in the morning. McLeods are living in Jón Einarson's house. She has a little girl. Her name is Elizabeth Slather.

All the snow is going now. Many men are using wagons as most of the snow is gone. We have been having good weather but if you step off the sidewalk, you get wet as it is very wet outside.

Doddi Thordarson had his own dog and never got all the way because he got played out on the way. A half-breed got the prize. His name was Campbell. One Icelander nearly got it, but he fell on a rail and hurt his foot so he had to give up running and lost the lead.

I think Hannes Kristjanson is going to get married to Ella Magnuson. He goes over to Freeman's three times a day with her, and has his meals there since his mother went away. She went to the coast and young Oli went with his father.

Well, dear brother, I hope you are in the best of health now and have not been wounded at all. Guðrún is coming home now so I think I will quit and go to feed the cow and sheep as it is 6:30 now. I will close now.

Your brother,
Wyatt Polson

Archie also received a letter from a young woman named Doris Bass, whom he met at the Mixer at the London Y.M.C.A in December. Doris lived at the Warwickshire Hotel. Now known as Bonham-Carter House, the Warwickshire Hotel was, beginning in 1912, a hostel for unmarried female staff at the Bourne and Hollingsworth Department Store in London.

Doris previously wrote to Archie, and even sent him a parcel, but her correspondence went unanswered. Doris alludes to enclosing a slip of paper in this letter, but it did not survive. Since there is no other record of correspondence with Doris, we can assume that her affections were not returned.

DORIS BASS
202 ROOM
TELEPHONE:
WARWICKSHIRE HOUSE
MUSEUM 2222
GOWER STREET
LONDON, W.C.
APR 8–17

My Dear Archie,

Just a few lines hoping this will find you in the best of health. I have been look-ing out for a letter from you every post, but have not had a line from you.

I sent you a parcel on the 22nd of last month. I hope that you have received it. Write and let me know when you get it.

I have nothing to write about as I have not had a letter from you asking for news. I sent my brother a parcel at the same time as I sent yours, it takes about two weeks for letters and parcels to reach him. I hope that he will receive his.

Well Archie, why have you not written to me for such a long time? What have I done? Have I offended you in any of my letters? If so, tell me.

We start closing at seven o'clock next week. Rather rotten I call it. That means eleven hours work. It is awful just now. We are rushed out all day, am getting quite fed up but I suppose that I must stick to it.

The weather is still very cold, but today, Sunday, the sun is shining and this afternoon I am going for a walk over Hampstead Heath. Coming with me, Archie?

I wish that you could. It is a ripping place. When you get leave, we will go there. When you get to the top of the heath, you can see for miles all around. It is really first rate and am quite sure that you will like it.

What do you think of the enclosed slip of paper? Now must really close. Happy to hear soon.

Best Love,
From Doris.

Elísabet with her arm resting on the shoulder of her mother, Þuriður Elísabet Jónsdóttir.

The Polson family in about 1912. FRONT ROW: Fjóla, Konnie and Lena.
MIDDLE ROW: Margrjét, Florence, Ágúst, Wyatt, Elísabet and Gústa.
THIRD ROW: Josie, Archie and Bonnie. Note that the younger girls are
wearing dresses made from the same bolt of cloth.

Archie as a baby.

Archie's confirmation photograph. He was fourteen years and wearing his first suit.

Archie prior to signing up for the army.

Archie with his friends just after they all signed up. He is second from the right, with Joe Daniel on his right and Ásmundur ("Mundi") Einarson on his left. Julius ("Julli") Stefanson is seated third from the left.

Archie's last visit to his beloved farm. Florence Paulson wrote the following on the back of the photograph: "After Archie joined the army, Stjana Orr took this picture of Archie in uniform at the corner of the house. [The house] had been vacant for many years."

The Gimli men of the 108th Battalion. They would soon head off for training at the Red Feather farm near Selkirk. Archie is in the centre of the front row. He has not as yet been issued a uniform. Ásmundur ("Mundi") Einarson, is at the right end of the second row, and Captain Jónas Jónasson is standing directly behind Archie. Julius ("Julli") Stefanson is in the back row, second from the left, and Pete Olson can be seen over the Captain's left shoulder. Captain Jónasson's rank was reduced to lieutenant when the 108th went to Camp Hughes.

Archie at Camp Hughes. Judging from his
gloves and his muddy boots, he has just returned
from a cross-country march.

Archie and his army pals while in leave from Camp Crowborough. Archie's hand written comments on the back refer to the roman numerals on the front: "I – my bed mate Forrest Jardine, II – myself, III – my friend Pte. S. Johnstone".

Photos like this provided the home audience with a heroic aspect to 'going over the top' at Vimy Ridge. NATIONAL ARCHIVE OF CANADA (NAC)

Archie's funeral with full military honours. The pallbearers stand on either side of the open grave, while the chaplain reads from the Bible and the officers give a final salute. The firing party stands at ease before firing the traditional three-volley salute.

MR. AND MRS. A. G. POLSON, 652 Goulding street, celebrated the 56th anniversary of their wedding Saturday. Both were born in Iceland, and came to Canada with their families as children. They were married in Winnipeg. Mrs. Polson was educated in North Dakota. They have nine children: Mrs. S. C. Ward, Winnipeg; Mrs. B. Bjarnason, of Langruth; Mrs. B. M. Paulson, of Arborg; Mrs. V. Bjarnason, of Langruth; Mrs. J. M. Jackson, Essendale, B.C.; Mrs. P. Goodman and Mrs. A. Goodman, of Winnipeg; Florence A., at home; R. W. Polson, of Lakt Francis, and J. K. Polson, of Winnipeg. A third son, Archibald, died of wounds overseas during the last war. There are 11 grandchildren and one great grandchild.

The announcement of Elísabet and Ágúst's 56th anniversary in 1944.

Winnipeg Free Press, 1944.

Florence's wedding in 1927. Photograph taken in front of 118 Emily
Street. BACK ROW, LEFT TO RIGHT: Lena, Wyatt, Florence, Björn M.
Paulson, Gústa. MIDDLE ROW, LEFT TO RIGHT: Frank Ward, Josie,
Valdimar Bjarnarson, Margrjét. FRONT ROW, LEFT TO RIGHT: Björn
Bjarnarson, Bonnie, Elísabet, Ágúst, Konnie, Fjóla.

Photos by Hugh Allan

Nine-layer Vinaterta is specialty of Mrs. Paul Goodman (l) of Winnipeg. At the right her mother, Mrs. Elisabet Polson, shows how to turn one of her Ponnukukur with the fingers.

ICELANDIC DISHES

Winnipeg cooks give Vinaterta and Ponnukukur recipes

WHEN Elisabet Polson left Skagafird in Iceland in 1876, she remembers there weren't any stoves on the island. The women used home-made utensils and cooked on large stone slabs, heated by fires beneath. Nowadays, in Winnipeg, where, at 84, she is one of the oldest in the settlement of 6,000 Icelanders, she has more up-to-date equipment but continues to cook traditional Icelandic dishes. Her daughter, Mrs. Paul Goodman, has written down the recipes and has learned the methods, although she has never been to Iceland.

festive occasions and as a dona-

Icelandic Lutheran Church, Mrs. Goodman makes a delicate Vinaterta, which is one of the best-known Icelandic desserts still made frequently in places like Winnipeg and Gimli, where another Icelandic settlement lives. The pastry for the Vinaterta (which means Wine Tart) is light, is rolled very thin and should be made a day in advance of baking, although Mrs. Goodman's recipe can be kept as long as a week. Another recipe given to me by Grandmother Polson is one for Ponnukukur, which means Pancakes.

Here are the good Icelandic

Elísabet and Lena tell about Icelandic cooking, *Winnipeg Tribune*, 1953.

PIONEER SPIRIT: Mrs. Elizabeth Polson, 89, of Winnipeg, kept a sharp eye and ear on proceedings at Gimli Monday. She was one of the original settlers, coming from Iceland in 1876. Next to her is Paul Finnbogason of Brandon, eldest of the five sons of Mrs. Olavia Finnbogson, the Maid of the Mountain. On his knee is niece Lenore Finnbogason.

Elísabet at her last Icelandic Festival in Gimli, *Winnipeg Free Press*, August, 1958.

CHAPTER SIX
A CASUALTY OF WAR

ON APRIL 2, 1917, THE CANADIAN ARTILLERY AT VIMY RIDGE commenced a general assault on the enemy's trenches. It lasted for a week, and culminated in the final attack on April 9. War historian Gerald Nicholson writes that the German forces described the onslaught by the Canadians as "the week of suffering" because their trenches and defensive works (presumably he meant their fortifications) were almost completely demolished.[36] It took several days to gain full control of the ridge, but the army's goal was achieved late on April 12.

The only record of an attempt by the Germans to reply to the Canadian shelling is a notation in the wartime diary of a Canadian soldier named John Newton, apparently written on April 6th, 1917: "Night alarm at 10 P.M. last night. The whole line woke up. Shells rained across— machine guns rattled—bedlam broke loose. Things settled down after half an hour, with the exception of the occasional rattle of machine guns and the regular night firing of artillery."[37]

Archie was wounded on April 5, likely during that exchange. The Polson family was first notified in a Night Lettergram dated April 11, 1917, the text handwritten in pencil.

CANADIAN PACIFIC R'Y CO.'S TELEGRAPH
NIGHT LETTERGRAM
G.N.W. OTTAWA, ONT   APRL. 11TH/17
AUGUST POLSON — GIMLI, MAN.

D.L.L. 7 – *Sincerely regret inform you 721948 Private Archibald John Polson infantry officially reported seriously ill*

Sixteen General Hospital, Letreport April eighth nineteen seventeen. Gunshot wound right thigh, arms. Will send further particulars when received.

Officer i.c. Records.

The whole family was distraught at the news, but no one more than Elísabet. She wrote to Archie on April 17, as soon as she obtained an address for him. In fact, she wrote two letters, one virtually the same as the other. German U-boats were a constant threat to Trans-Atlantic shipping during the war, and Elísabet was wise to send two letters as a precaution. The letter reproduced below is the lengthier of the two.

Elísabet mentions Miss Denison is a woman who was staying with Nina Polson at her home on Rose Street. While her identity is unknown, the Denisons were an influential family in Manitoba, so Miss Denison would have been well connected.

Elísabet also comments that Margrjét does not wish to teach Galicians. By this time, many Ukrainian immigrants from the province of Galicia had homesteaded in the Interlake. In the early days, the Icelanders and the Ukrainians did not always get along well. The Icelanders took pride, occasionally to the point of hubris, in their intellectual pursuits, while the early Ukrainian settlers tended to be rough around the edges. The friction has long since subsided, and intermarriage is now common.

GIMLI, MAN.

APRIL 17 1917

My Darling Boy,

Oh how will I commence this letter dearest Archie as we are all thinking of you and pray for your recovery and that you will be able to come back to us again dearest boy of mine. Your Father got a lettergram saying you were seriously ill and wounded. Oh how we all felt sad, but we hope for the best and as I said before, pray to God you will be spared us.

Your father is so angsious [sic] about you as we all are. Oh, if we could only be near you and help to nurse you my own darling boy. And all your friends, and it seems everybody here is your friend as the whole Town seems angsious [sic] about you and express their regrets. If only we could be sure this and other letters could reach you and we could feel we could do something for you my own darling boy. We are all pretty well at home here but all thinking of you. Now the boys in the 223 Battalion are expected to go any day now. Mr. and Mrs. Tergesen, and Inga and Joe, are going to bid them goodbye. [Archie's friend, their son Pete, had signed up with the 223rd Battalion.] Your sister, Margrjét, is going to teach in Inga's place so Inga can go, but Margrjét does not like to teach Galicians she has found that out. Old Mrs. Saffrin said she had just been sick when she heard you were wounded and so were others. I'm not going to say much about you myself but there is one thing. I want to be worthy to be a mother of a brave soldier boy. Oh how proud we all are of you, my own brave boy.

I have had letters from Miss Denison at Auntie's, and Mrs. Flint, Mr. and Mrs. Hadkinsson [Archie's former teacher] and Josie and Bonnie, and so many phones all cheering me in the hope I will get you back my darling Archie (that name is sweet to me). Núni and Uncle and Johanna are staying with us at present, but do not know how long they will be here. Uncle has some jobs of fence paintings in town here. He has fixed Tergesen's Store just fine. Everybody admires it. What do you think that Hannes Kristjanson is married to Ella Magnusson? They got married last Sunday and Albert, his brother, came down and married them. Gumbi and Jóna Arason asked him. They were married at Johann Freemans'. Benedikt Freemans is getting better. Mundi Johnson and his wife are moving (I mean the barber) and Ásbjörn Eggertson is renting his house. Maud Bristow has bought Hadkinsson's house and will move in there soon.

Well my darling boy, I can't think of much news for this letter as I can only think of you. I'm going to send Mrs. Flint's letter to you for you to read so as to make this feel more like a letter. All the children are standing around me while I'm writing this to you. God be with you and I pray him to spare you if it his Blessed will that I might clasp you in my arms.

Your own loving mother,
E. Polson

After Archie was wounded, he was taken to No. 30 Casualty Clearing Station located in Aubigny-en-Artois, about nineteen kilometers from the

Front. Wade Davis in his book *Into The Silence: The Great War, Mallory and the Conquest of Everest* wrote about Casualty Clearing Stations:

> Located out of immediate threat of shell fire, yet as close to the Front as possible, the ccs was both a hospital and a clearinghouse. There the medical teams, generally eight surgeons working around the clock, two to a six hour shift, separated by triage those strong enough to be immediately evacuated by rail to the base hospitals from those whose injuries necessitate immediate surgery. A third cohort comprised those so severely wounded that there was no hope. These were tagged in red and placed in a moribund ward where they might be sedated and bathed, and comforted by nurses who did what they could to shield the lads from the inevitability of their fate. [...] The stress on the medical officers at a casualty clearing station was intense and unrelenting. [...] Their smocks drenched in blood, with the nauseating scent of sepsis and cordite and human excrement fouling the operating room, they cut and sliced and sawed and cauterized wounds of a sort that they never would have known in ordinary practice. [...] Shrapnel did the most damage, jagged splinters of steel, red hot, driving debris and bits of uniform and the flesh of battlefield cadavers deep into wounds.[38]

No. 30 ccs was a British facility. A Canadian ccs had recently relocated in Aubigny from Bailleul, but it may have already had a full complement of patients. Since writing was a challenge for Archie due to his wounds, caregivers did their best to contact Elísabet for him, and to comfort her to the extent that they could. The following hand-written letter from Chaplain W. E. Bates of No. 30 ccs took several weeks to reach the family.

6/4/17.

Dear Mrs Polson

Pte. Polson your son wishes me to write and tell you that he is lying here in Hospital wounded. He is very brave and bears his pain manfully. Unfortunately he has lost his right arm but is confident that he will get well, and hopes that you will not worry overmuch on his account. He is lying at present in No. 30 Casualty Clearing Station, from which he will in all

probability be moved shortly. As soon as he is settled (he hopes in England)
he will write and acquaint you, so that you may write to him there.

I'm sure you will like to know the above in order that you may pray for
his speedy recovery.

I am,
Yours Truly,
Wm. E. Bates (Chaplain to the Forces)

Archie may not have had the benefit of anesthesia when his arm was
amputated. A Canadian anesthetist who treated wounded soldiers at the
Battle of the Somme has been quoted as saying: "In severe action, a CCS
is very busy and I cannot imagine any place where a skilled anesthetist
would be more useful. A CCS cannot, however, afford to have much cum-
bersome apparatus as when the army moves, it moves too."[39]

Archie was transferred from No. 30 CCS to another British facility,
No. 16 General Hospital in Le Tréport, a small fishing port on the English
Channel. Le Tréport was also the location of Canada's No. 2 General
Hospital. Together they comprised a massive tent city. A nursing sister
at No. 16 General Hospital hand wrote to Elísabet.

16 GENERAL HOSPITAL
B. E. F.
APRIL 10TH.17
Dear Mrs. Polson
I am indeed sorry to tell you that your son, Pte. Polson of S. Can. M.G. Coy.
has been admitted to this hospital wounded. His wounds are serious & we
hope that he will make satisfactory progress. He came here two days ago & I
am pleased to tell you that he has improved greatly.

I will write again in a few days & then perhaps can give you some idea
when he will be able to travel to England.

At present he cannot write himself, as his right arm was amputated before
reaching here.

I don't want you to worry. I have every hope that he will recover.

Promising to write again & with my sincerest sympathy and best wishes. He sends his love and he is such a good patient.

With best wishes Yours sincerely,
V. G. Bach.
Sister

It did not take long for Archie to hear from his Member of Parliament, George Bradbury, Conservative M.P. for Selkirk.[40] While Bradbury was the organizer and first Lieutenant Colonel of the 108th Battalion, he had not accompanied the battalion overseas, likely due to his parliamentary duties.

CANADA
HOUSE OF COMMONS
OTTAWA
APRIL 13TH, 1917.
PTE. ARCHIBALD JOHN POLSON
NO. 721948, CANADIAN EXPEDITIONARY FORCE,
16 GENERAL HOSPITAL,
LETREPORT, FRANCE.

Dear Polson,
I am in receipt this morning of notification from the Military Department, to the effect that you are confined to the hospital suffering from gun shot wound to the right thigh and arms. I assure you that you have my sincere sympathy, and I trust that before this reaches you, you will be well on the way to recovery.

While I sympathize with your suffering, yet I feel I must congratulate you in having been permitted to discharge the valuable services that you have in defence of our country. Such services as you and other have been rendering will not soon be forgotten. If there is anything I can do to alleviate your suffering, or assist you, I would be glad to know.

You will understand I am very much interested in all the old 108th Battalion, and desire to keep in touch with them.

Trusting that this will find you well on the way to recovery, I am,

Yours sincerely,
Geo. H. Bradbury

In early 1917, public support for the war in Canada was at low ebb, and casualties spiked with every major battle, most recently more than 24,000 wounded or dead at the Battle of the Somme over the course of two months in the autumn of 1916. Army recruitment was down, and there was ongoing controversy about the need to invoke conscription.

Then in April, the attack on Vimy Ridge took place and in just a few days, Canada suffered 10,602 more casualties—3,598 were killed. The scope of the losses is rendered even more significant when one considers that Canada's population at the time was less than eight million.

Nevertheless, the government and the military proclaimed a monumental success at Vimy Ridge. A *Manitoba Free Press* headline in its Tuesday, April 10 edition told of a "Brilliant Attack" that resulted in the capture of the ridge in a half hour, with only "light" casualties.[41] There were, in fact, three main headlines on the front page that day: "British smash through German line; Canadians storm famous Vimy Ridge", "Brilliant Attack of Canadians Results in Capture of Famous Vimy Ridge in Half Hour–Casualties Light", and "Big Gains Made On Fifteen Mile Front at Arras".

A story reported:

> Heavy casualties have been inflicted on the Germans, and in addition, prisoners running into the thousands—5,816 have already been counted—and great quantities of war material were captured. The operations are still in progress. The victors' casualties are reported to have been slight.[42]

In a headline on the following day, the newspaper announced the capture of 11,000 German prisoners. On Thursday, the Minister of Militia was quoted as saying:

> After such a grand victory, which is sure to go down in history as one of the great achievements of the history of our country, surely young men who have hesitated about enlisting in the overseas forces will, under such inspiration, heed the call of their fellow-countrymen to 'come and help', and at once put

their names on the scroll of honor, and in this way feel like they acted like men when the freedom and liberties of their country were threatened.[43]

The true extent of the casualties was not reported until the following Monday, buried on page 4. If all of this was a public relations strategy (abetted by a compliant press), then it was a successful one.

Canada has recently endured the Afghan conflict, which lost public support when casualties mounted. There were 157 combat deaths over nine years in Afghanistan, and 636 were wounded in battle. It is difficult therefore for the contemporary observer to understand that the perceived triumph at Vimy Ridge overshadowed its terrible cost.

In the weeks following Vimy Ridge, there would have been 10,602 night lettergrams like the one sent to Ágúst Polson. Yet, just over a month after the attack, *Manitoba Free Press* reported 100,000 people lined the streets of Winnipeg to witness the Decoration Day parade.[44] While this attendance figure seems inflated (the total population of Winnipeg according to the 1916 census was 163,000), there can be little doubt that the crowd that day was large. The parade, according to *Manitoba Free Press*, included, in addition to a throng of dignitaries, 2,000 men of the Canadian Expeditionary Force awaiting their call for overseas, and 1,000 returned soldiers.

At a memorial service following the parade, a local clergyman made a pro-war speech which gives a sense of the militaristic attitude of those who supported the war effort, and were emboldened by the success at Vimy Ridge. What follows are excerpts from the homily that day:

> We are mindful […] of the large and rapidly growing number of neighbours and friends whose hearts are bowed down with grief because of the message which the cable has wrought, and to them, all we whom the war has not yet so closely touched, extend affectionate and grateful sympathy.
>
> We marvel often at the spirit which they show in their bereavement. "We do not grudge [sic] him," said one father, whose only son was taken. "I am glad to be able to make such a contribution to the cause," said another, the fateful telegram in his hand and his eyes filled with tears. When we hear words like these we understand in part the fortitude of the lads at the front.

And these fathers and mothers are right. God has taken their boys at their best, in the very Christ-like act of laying down their lives for others, and immoderate sorrow should never follow a worthy sacrifice.

The homily climaxed with this rallying cry:

Our boys at Vimy Ridge moved forward to the attack at the break of dawn. We believe that will prove to be symbolic of the dawn of a new day here that shall reveal a better Canada, [the] most fitting monument of those that fall so that she may rise.[45]

In any letters to Archie, including two from his elder sisters, there is no suggestion of a loss of confidence in the government, the military, or the war effort.

Josie was Archie's sister, and at twenty-eight she was the eldest of the ten Polson children. She wrote to Archie on April 19th. Bonnie wrote to Archie on the same day and told him that Josie was very upset, yet Josie's letter comes across as rather harsh and uncaring. Some people have difficulty expressing their emotions, and apparently Josie was one of them. When she wrote to her brother, she resorted, almost as a defence mechanism, to acting the big sister and telling him not to feel sorry for himself, because his plight could be so much worse.

By this time, Josie was married to Frank Ward, and she was pregnant. Life was difficult and demanding for the young couple. They were homesteading on marginal land near the remote hamlet of Erinview, along the shores of Shoal Lake in Manitoba's western Interlake region. Josie was a hawk about the war and may have felt guilty because Frank had not signed up. Given their trying circumstances, not enlisting was probably the wise choice, but once again Josie does not express herself well. Frank later served in the army, likely having been conscripted.

ERINVIEW, MAN.
APRIL 19TH, 1917
My dear Archie,
Did you think I was dead, or something like that, when I have not written oftener? Well, I am very much alive, but writing seems out of the question lately with me.

Needless to say, I am terribly put out about your recent experience. But there is no good sending you a letter of lamentations, is it my dear? And best to be as cheerful under the circumstances, and be oh, so thankful that you did not get into the hands of the Germans as a prisoner—also that you were not gassed, and oh so thankful that you still have your sight.

I just got the address yesterday of the hospital that you are in, so I did not waste much time, did I? It's good that you're in hospital in France, and I'm sure the nurses must be nice, but how busy they must be. According to the papers, there were 5,000 casualties in the great drive to Vimy Ridge; at first 15,000 was quoted.

I'll bet Bonnie wishes she were there, and doing her bit. Oh, didn't I wish that I were a man when I got the news about you. I'd have gone right straight, with such hatred in my heart, and full of revenge.

Bill [Josie's brother-in-law] feels it keenly that he was never accepted-and it's utterly impossible now as he was ruptured again just lately. Frank is talking again about going, but at present it is utterly out of the question till the hay is up. Ted [a second brother-in-law] is still in England, and in each letter, wishing it were his last week, and that his turn will come soon to be called to the Front. He says that it's rotten luck to come all the way from the Yukon to get there, and then be held up in England.

Do you remember Bobbie Aitkins who used to chum with Rose St. Bay? He was very fair, was a Lieut[enant] in the 78th. He was killed in the big drive. I see by the papers that one of the Andrews boys has returned. I don't know whether it's Ray or Bert.

We have had rotten weather—a few nice days and then snow, then thaw and misty weather, everything is terribly slushy. Rob has not ventured taking his Tin Lizzy out yet. He has had a garage built at last. It's east of the old house and due south of Balderstone's shanty.

The geese have been quite plentiful and large flocks have been passing over, all because it's closed season for them, which is very aggravating.

Of course you hear from home regularly. Had a letter from Noonie. She has left Riverton and doesn't know where they will live and was at mother's at time of writing. She tells me Hannes Kristjanson and Ella Magnuson were married.

His brother Albert officiated. They at home once attended a service Albert had, but were not so greatly impressed that they wished to change churches.

What do you think of Dad working at Tergesen's? I hope it's a change for the better.

Did anyone tell you of Grannie Collie's death? She had been failing since Jan. 9th and passed away very peacefully on March 28. Mrs. Ward was in for the funeral and also on two previous occasions, once to see Grannie and relieve Nora and Aunt Nell at nursing her, and again to see Aunt [illegible] who came and nursed Grannie the last six or eight weeks. You'll remember her, Mrs. Mitchell, who was out here when you visited Erinview the first time.

Mrs. Ward and Jean have colds; otherwise all is well. The boys are cutting oak into cordwood for next winter's sale. This will have to do for the present. I will write soon again.

I sincerely hope that you will soon be on the road to recovery, my dear. Keep up a stout heart, Old Boy. Keep up your old faith. Remember there is One who will never fail you. Remember how many thousands are worse off than you. We will soon have you home once again, and there will be a jolly gathering. Heaps of love from one and all.

Lovingly, your sister,
Josie Ward.

Archie had always been Bonnie's favourite, as one can tell immediately from her letter of April 19. In this letter, she wrote that it was eleven days since Archie was wounded. No clear date had been provided to the family, so this appears to be a supposition.

Bonnie was in training to become a nurse, and she wrote the letter at the end of her night shift at The Logan Annex, also known as The Old Coffee House. "The Annex" was a convalescent facility affiliated with Winnipeg General Hospital, now the Winnipeg Health Sciences Centre.

Bonnie would go on to have a long and distinguished career as a nurse, primarily in Langruth, Manitoba where she settled. In 1969, the Province of Manitoba presented her with a Good Citizenship Award "for her work in the nursing service to Indians, Métis and white people over the past 50 years".[46]

My own darling Archie,

This is now the eleventh day since you were so seriously wounded, and I pray and rely on God's mercy that you are on the safe road to recovery. Dear boy, I cannot tell you how we all felt when we received the night lettergram. Of course, we should have been expecting it, but we always hoped that nothing would happen to you, our dearly beloved boy. We all felt heart-broken, but tried to be very brave. Archie dear, I am sure that you are getting better, for surely we would have heard if you were any worse. And Archie, put all of your will into force, for the stronger the will, the speedier the recovery.

Josie was very upset, perhaps more so because she is not well. But believe me, we are all brave, and are sure that with God's help and our prayers, and your strong will, you will recover and be back home with us once more. Your picture appeared in Lögberg and the Free Press today. And I feel awfully proud of my brother who was wounded for the cause. But believe me, I feel very indignant when I see young men on the street in civvies, who should be in khaki, but who are only shirkers. And I think that because of these shirkers, my brother and other girls' brothers are fighting desperately.

Well, Archie boy, I am still on night duty at the Annex. I am getting more used to it, so like it a little better now, in spite of the majority of the patients who, as I told you before, are not of the better class as far as character goes.

Auntie [Nina] has been receiving numerous letters from Frank. She had as many as four one day. This being due to the tie up in the mail here and abroad. In one of his letters he was reminding Auntie of the fact that he was broke and wanted, among other things, to buy chocolate to send to you. I am so glad that you two boys are still so fond of each other, though parted for the time being. Each of you in your letters seems to be thinking of the other, which is lovely.

Miss Denison certainly has been good to us. She has been the biggest comfort for she knows so much about things over there, and has told us exactly how things are. She has written to London to get particulars, and knows just where to write. Mamma was going to cable but Miss D. said cabling was most unsatisfactory for it had been tried often with poor results.

Runie Thompson just told me her mother and sister, Emma, had just packed and sent off a parcel to you. I thought it was so good of them. I hope that you will get it, and eat and enjoy its contents.

I had just written a short letter and started another when I heard the news, neither of which I sent, so I will just enclose them without further summary, but will let this letter be the grand finale of them all.

Everyone is asking about you, Archie. Of course, they are seeing who and what you are, Archie Polson, the best and noblest boy under the sun. And please hurry up and get better. Oh, what wouldn't I give to be a military nurse? Just think, I might be nursing you now, dear, if I'd entered the hospital about three years earlier. I hope that the nurses and doctors will be good to you. Of course, they couldn't be otherwise, but still there are different degrees of goodness and patience. Tell me about your nurse and the other nurses when you are able to write, dear. There will be no one more interested than your old Bon.

I had such a nice dream day before yesterday that I called mamma up on the phone, and told her about it. I dreamt you were here in the General Hospital and that I was nursing you, and you were so bright and well, that is to say, as well as you could be, my Archie. I felt so happy when I awoke, and for the rest of the day, I felt like a new person.

Well, Archie boy, 'tis time for me to cease, for the morning work is all to be done yet before I go off for seven, and then to bed, for I am a wee bit sleepy.

Goodbye, my darling.
I am your caring,
Bon.

A second Lettergram was sent to Archie's father, Ágúst, dated April 25, 1917, advising that Archie is "no longer seriously ill."

CANADIAN PACIFIC R'Y CO.'S TELEGRAPH
NIGHT LETTERGRAM
OTTAWA, ONT 25 APRL /17
AUGUST POLSON GIMLI, MAN.

DF 44. – *Cable received today states 721948 Private Archibald John Polson Infantry officially reported as no longer seriously ill. Sixteen general hospital,*

Letreport, April twenty first nineteen seventeen.

Officer 1/o Records.

Elísabet was ecstatic over the news. She had been to hell and back, first thinking that Archie might soon die, but now she had to come to grips with the prospect that he would be disabled for the rest of his life. She was destined to vacillate between hope and despair for months.

GIMLI, MAN.
APRIL 26, 1917.
My dearest Archie,
What joyful news we got this morning from Ottawa, telling us that you were declared no more seriously ill.

My, it did us a world of good, so we are all thinking of the time when we will have you with us again. Margrjét says she will be your secretary for everything but your love letters. She is now practising copying the telegram that came today to send to our friends that are so angsious [sic] about you, my darling boy.

Poor Bonnie, she was simply sick first when she heard of your injury, but this is joyful news to her, as it is to us. Everybody is asking about you here. I wonder if you have got any of our letters. I got two letters I sent last to Crowborough. I got them from the Dead Letter Office and sent them off again. I hope you will get them.

I know that you will try to make your time pleasant as possible, in spite of all the pain, which I know you must go through. We certainly have much to thank our Heavenly Father for—all His mercies and in giving you back to us again, as we all hope for and feel will come to pass. When we get you home to us, how sweet that will be for us all.

My darling, how thankful I am to you for your presence of mind to ask the chaplain [Chaplain Bates] to think of me, and to write to me. We were so very, very glad to receive the letter in spite of that sad news of you losing your right arm.

We do not mind that, as long as God will spare you to us. Little Jón Thordarson has been as thoughtful as if you were his big brother. I am not writing for the rest of the family as they are all going to write to you. If you can get anyone to write for you, then tell me what we can do for you. I sent you seven dollars in March, and I sent it as you directed.

Well, my darling boy, I will not write more this time as I am not sure this will get to you as I am using the address the telegram gave us or was dated from. God give you strength and restore you to health and back to us, your loving mother, father, brothers and sisters.

E. Th. Polson.

The last letter sent to Elísabet from France was handwritten note from a military chaplain at No. 16 General Hospital. The letter was written on April 23, at about the time that Archie was transferred to hospital in England. Elísabet did not receive the letter until May 18.

16 GENERAL HOSPITAL
B.E.F.
FRANCE. APRIL 23RD 1917.
Dear Mrs Polson,
I have seen much of your dear son in Ward 3 of this hospital here, & he asked me to drop you a line a few days ago. He has lost his right arm—you will be grieved to hear that. But he has otherwise completely recovered, and looks as well as one can be in bed. We have talked together often as he is in excellent spirits. Last Sunday I was administering the Holy Communion to two other wounded soldiers &, as he had expressed his willingness to do the same, he received the Sacrament with them.

They were all badly wounded, but are quite well now & will be travelling to England very soon—if they did not go last evening on the train that left yesterday. This is a fine hospital on the French coast & they get the best of nursing.

Yours sincerely,
W.J. Grarell
Chaplain to the Forces.
C. of E.
[Church of England]

CHAPTER SEVEN

THE LONG RECUPERATION

ARCHIE WAS SENT INITIALLY TO THE MILITARY HOSPITAL at Stepping Hill, Stockport, England, located in the Midlands, near Manchester. He was visited by volunteers from the Red Cross, most notably a lady named Mrs. Annie E. Paine, who hand-wrote a letter of encouragement to his family.

APRIL 25/17
Dear Mrs Polson,
Today as Canadian
Red Cross visitor to Stepping Hill Hospital, Stockport, I visited your son Arch. J. Polson. He tells me that he is feeling much better and has much less pain, I shall see him often, and if I can do anything for him I shall be only too pleased. If all does not go well, I will let you know—he looks much better than many of our men who I have seen after amputations.

He will receive every attention at the hospital—if there is any matter you would like attended to for him will you let me know. Hoping you will not worry.

Believe me,
In great haste,
Yours very truly,
(Mrs) Annie E. Paine.

There seems to have been a misunderstanding between Mrs. Paine and the Canadian Red Cross over who should be communicating to Elísabet. On May 1, 1917, Constance Scott of the Red Cross sent an update on Archie's condition, apparently arising from Mrs. Paine's report of her visit. Over the next several months, there were regular updates, handwritten on a standard form and signed in the name of Ms. Scott, but none were written in her hand.

Ms. Scott dictated the reports to a large pool of writers, or delegated the reporting function. Either way, she retained ultimate responsibility, and, given the size of her staff, there were a great many convalescent soldiers.

CANADIAN RED CROSS SOCIETY,
14/16 COCKSPUR STREET,
LONDON S.W. 1.
INFORMATION BUREAU
1.5.17.

Dear Madam

I BEG TO INFORM YOU THAT *Pte. J. Polson 721.948 2nd M.G. Co.*
WHO IS NOW AT *Stepping Hill, Hospital, Stockport, England*
has been seen at the above hospital by our Red Cross visitor who reports that he has been admitted suffering from wounds in his thigh & arms. I am so sorry that he has had to have his right arm amputated. He is feeling more comfortable & so glad to be over here from France. I only wish I could have sent you more details, but one visitor only reports that although Private Polson is still very ill he is certainly better than he was on his arrival in hospital. His cousins [Frank Polson and Mundi Einarson] have been sent for, to come & see him, so that will help cheer him up a little. You may rest assured that he is having the very best care & attention & any extra comforts he may want will be sent to him from the Red Cross. We will write to you again soon as we receive our next report. One visitor will see him regularly while he is in hospital. With good wishes for a speedy recovery.

Yours truly
Constance Scott
D.S.P.

A few days later, Mrs. Paine visited Archie again, and wrote to Elísabet.

MAY 5TH/17

Dear Mrs. Polson.

With great pleasure I write to tell you that your boy Arch. J. is making good progress, his wounds are many & bad, but the improvement in him is great. I was pleased to see such an improvement. He is very bright & all things possible are being done for him. He has commenced to write to you, but finds it rather hard work with his left hand.

Yours very truly
(Mrs.) Annie Paine.

Once again, Constance Scott of the Red Cross reported to Elísabet on the most recent visit by Mrs. Paine.

INFORMATION BUREAU
CANADIAN RED CROSS SOCIETY,
14/16 COCKSPUR STREET,
LONDON S.W. 1.
8.5.17
IN ANSWERING PLEASE REPEAT NAME, NUMBER,
AND BATTALION OF SOLDIER.

Dear Madam

I BEG TO INFORM YOU THAT Pte. J. Polson No. 721.948 2nd M.G. Co. WHO IS NOW AT Stepping Hill Military Hospital, Stockport, Cheshire, England has again been seen by our authorised representative who reports that Pte. Polson is very much better, though he is still in a critical condition. A parcel was sent to him from that Department of this office which he was very pleased with. We hope very much, that as Pte. Polson is better, he will continue to make steady improvement.

Yours very truly,
Constance Scott
Per K.W.

The parcel mentioned above was likely the one referred to in this typed letter from the 108th Auxiliary.

As referred to in the letter of May 5 from Mrs. Paine, Archie started to write a letter to Elísabet shortly after arriving at Stockport. He was determined to demonstrate that he was on the road to recovery, but it was a daunting task. Not only was Archie forced to write with his left hand for the first time in his life, he had to do so while lying flat on his back. Despite these obstacles, his penmanship is quite legible, and the letter is remarkably long—twelve pages have been recovered but there may have been more. It was written over the span of several days. Elísabet did not receive Archie's letter for many weeks.

Notably, Archie reports that he has told his cousin, Frank Polson, to stay away from France. Frank did go "on draft" a few months later, but it is unclear whether he saw action. Archie also mentions having seen his friend, Julli Stefanson, in late March. Julli participated in the advance at Vimy Ridge and his date of death is listed as April 9, 1917. Julli's body was never found. He was likely vaporized or blown to pieces by a shell. An alternative is that Julli was buried alive when a shell exploded nearby.

WARD B2,
STEPPING HILL HOSPITAL,
HAZEL GROVE, STOCKPORT,
ENGLAND.
MAY 3RD, 1917.

Dear Mother,

This looks like child's writing as I am writing with my left hand and I am lying in bed. It is slow work as this is the first letter I have written since I was wounded. I was three weeks in a hospital in France before I came to England. I am getting along nicely. It is just a matter of time before my wounds heal. In the meantime, I am well looked after. I expect that you have received several letters from nurses and ministers telling you how I was getting along. About three ministers and one nursing sister promised to write to you. I have not received any letters for a month as I have not written to my company to let them know where to forward my letters to. I expect Frank will come to see me one of these days.

MAY 4TH FRIDAY

I started this letter yesterday morning before breakfast, but did not finish it as Frank arrived just after breakfast. He is going to stay until Sunday. You can imagine how glad I was to see him.

He told me that Mundi has been sent to France. I never really thought that the army would ever send him across. Frank heard that Ingi Thordarson had been killed, but I am not sure that it is true. I saw Ingi and Sveinbjorn Pallson in France about March 15th or 20th, and also some other 108th boys that I knew. I saw Julli Stefanson about a week later, but he was not in the same battalion as Ingi.

Ingi might have been killed since I saw him. Such a thing could easily happen. Of course, his people would be notified immediately. This is an English hospital, but there are a few Canadians here, although they are in other wards.

So far I have been the only Canadian in this ward but this morning a new bunch of patients came in and there was a Canadian put into this ward. He is really a Yankee, but he joined a Halifax battalion and has been with the Canadians at the front.

I think most of Icelandic boys of the 108th are gone to France. Frank tells me that Joe Daniel had been on draft, but had not been sent because he was too young. It is now 3 p.m. and I have just had an inoculation in my left arm.

MAY 5TH SATURDAY

It is about 8 A.M. now and I have just had my breakfast. Frank slept here at the hospital night before last, but yesterday all the extra beds were filled with new patients. So yesterday, he got a room in a private house where he will sleep the remaining nights of his stay here. Frank will be going back to Shorncliffe tomorrow. Frank told me that Dad was working at Tergesen's. I was surprised when he told me. I have not received any letters for over a month. I am going to write to my company and let them know where to forward my mail to. Very likely there's a parcel waiting for me somewhere.

MONDAY MAY 7TH

Frank left Saturday afternoon. He thought he could stay till Sunday, but when he looked at his pass he saw that he had to be back Sunday morning. He had to leave here Saturday afternoon as it is a long journey. Well, dear mother, I have not much more news to tell you. It is about time I finished it and had it mailed.

How does dad like working at Tergesen's? Why did he quit s & t? Tell him not to mind though I don't write to him, because this letter is to him as well as to you.

I suppose you know by this time that I lost my right arm in the Great War. However, I am getting along fine. When I get better, I will get an artificial arm and when I get home, I will be able to be useful even if I am shy an arm. I'll be looking for a job when I get back to Canada.

This war is going to hit our old home town harder than I ever expected. I am afraid that some of the boys from home will never come back. I told Frank to stay away from France as long as he could, and not be too anxious to get there. There is a saying amongst some of the boys in the trenches that "it's better to be a living coward than a dead hero."

I have not written to Mrs. Tyler since I came here, but I will as soon as I can. I find it awkward to write in bed with my left hand, and I don't write much at a time. By the way, Frank told me that he had received two parcels from the Daughters of the Empire. I haven't got any from them yet, and I thought that they might send me one for a change. Maybe they will send me one when they hear that I have done my bit. It makes a fellow sore to think that he has been forgotten.

TUESDAY MAY 8TH

I think I'll finish this letter today. By the way, I was wounded by a German shell which burst right beside me. I am lucky to be alive at all. There was a young chap standing in front of me at the time, and he was killed on the spot. I felt so sorry for him because he was so young. He was only about 17 or 18.

How is Bonnie getting on? I suppose she will worry her head about her soldier brother just because he is wounded. Tell her she need not worry, because I'm not dead yet, not by a long way. "There's life in the old dog yet." And what's more, I'll be in Canada at the end of the summer or early fall.

When I get better, I will be sent to a place where artificial limbs are made to get a new arm. I will likely stay there until I get used to it, and learn how to use it. You need not worry about me.

I think I would like a small parcel. I would like some Player's cigarettes, a package of Old Chum tobacco, a plug of T & B Smoking tobacco and some chocolates and nut bars. I want to give Frank the package of Old Chum and send Mundi the plug of T & B. I wish you would send me one of my photos, if you have any left. If you send me cake or tarts, I am afraid it would spoil on the way as it takes the letters and parcels such a long time to get here.

I received a letter from Loa Sigurdson when I was in France, but I have lost her address. Give her my regards when you see her, and remember me to all my friends (not forgetting my old friend, Sarah Sveinson).

Give my love to all relatives. I wrote to Uncle John and to Aunt Annie when I was in France, but have not heard from them since. How is old Maggie getting on? Remember me to her. When you write be sure and tell me all the news.

There is a lady who lives near here who visits the Canadians quite often [Mrs. Paine] and she sometimes brings me fruit and cigarettes. She always brings me something. She is a representative of the Canadian Red Cross Society. She visits the Canadians and sends in reports of what we want.

I have received four parcels from the Can. Red Cross. The first was a bag containing useful articles such as shaving outfit, hair brush, chocolate, gum, etc. and a copy of the Free Press. The other parcels contained fruit, cigarettes, chocolate and another copy of the Free Press. Mrs. Johnson, the lady Frank stayed with when he was here, has been to see me twice. She is going to come and see me as often as she can. Visiting days are Wednesday.

At this point, the letter ends. The remainder appears to have been lost. The next report from the Red Cross was dated May 14, 1917. It came from Constance Scott, although it appears to have been written hurriedly, and was written in yet another hand. Good progress is reported.

INFORMATION BUREAU MAY 14–17
CANADIAN RED CROSS SOCIETY,
14/16 COCKSPUR STREET,
LONDON S.W. 1.
IN ANSWERING PLEASE REPEAT NAME, NUMBER,
AND BATTALION OF SOLDIER.

Dear Madam
I BEG TO INFORM YOU THAT *Pte. J. Polson No. 721,948 2nd* M.G. *Co.* WHO IS NOW AT *Stepping Hill, Hospital, Stockport–Cheshire–England– was visited again a few days ago. We are glad to tell you that our Visitor reports Pte. Polson to be making good progress, and he is cheerful & contented.*

Hoping this may continue.
Yours truly,
Constance Scott
p. p. GTS.

On May 16, 1917, a friend of Archie, Lolla Jónasson, wrote a sweet letter to Archie. She was a school teacher, which in those days required only one year at Normal School after graduation from high school.

Lolla was teaching in Framnes, a hamlet located about 160 kilometers north of Gimli. As in the case of many Interlake communities, its name had an Icelandic derivation. Framnes no longer exists.

Lolla reports that her brother was with the 223rd Battalion, which was a largely-Icelandic group assembled in early 1916. Archie's friend, Pete Tergesen, was also in the 223rd. The battalion sailed to France in May of 1917. It was absorbed into the 11th Reserve Battalion upon arrival and saw action in several battles including Hill 70, Passchendaele and Amiens. Pete Tergesen was injured in a mustard gas attack. His respiratory tract and lungs were so badly burned that he spent the rest of his life as an invalid. In despair, Pete became a recluse and an alcoholic.

Oblivious to all of that, Lolla's letter, like those from Archie's sisters, includes no suggestion of any loss of support for the war effort. In fact, the opposite appears to be true. The fate of Lolla's brother is unknown.

FRAMNES, MAN.
MAY 16, 1917.
Dear Archie,

I cannot tell you how sad I was to hear of the great affliction that you have lately experienced. I wish that I was powerful enough to offer you some consolation, but it must come from a higher power than mine. Still, you may be content to know that you could not refuse to do your duty to your country. When great sorrows like yours are met and overcome, then we are able to judge the courage of the sufferer.

I hope that you are getting along well, and before many weeks will be home again with us. We will all be heartily glad to have our boys back, and proud to know that they have done their duty. We that are safe at home are heartily thankful for the great work our boys are doing for us. It is hard for us to realize what great hardships and horrors they must go through.

I would like to tell you some news, but I know that your people write to you often, and tell you about the most important happenings such as Hannes and Ella M. getting married.

I am teaching school out here, and have a nice bunch of children. We were very busy on Monday, Arbor Day, making our school garden, and tidying up. Jóna is teaching at a school four miles from mine. She has been with me three weekends in succession, so I guess that it is my turn next. It is very nice to be able to see each other so often.

I heard from Jónas a few days ago. His letter was dated April 29th, and that morning they had just reached Halifax. I guess that they are all, the 223rd, over in England now.

Baldur is working at the munitions shops in Transcona.

Goodbye, Archie.

Sincerely hoping that you will recover very soon.

Your friend,
Lolla Jónasson

When Elísabet wrote to Archie on May 19, she reported that she had three letters from France. Those would be the letters from Chaplain Bates, Nurse Bach and Chaplain Grarell. She had also received the first letters from Mrs. Paine and the Red Cross. She had yet to receive Archie's letter of May 3 but, in any event, had gone from devastation to cautious optimism.

GIMLI, MAY 19, 1917.

My Darling Boy,

Oh, what a rejoicing here last night. We got one letter from Chaplain Grarell from France, as well as a card from your hospital that you are in from Mrs. Annie Paine, and one from the Canadian Red Cross society.

In the last letter I am told that your cousins have been sent for, and I am thankful for that as I know that it will cheer you up, and help you to get better. I have sent letters to France, but I suppose that you have not got them at all.

My last letter I sent to Mrs. Tyler, and I am sure that she will forward it to you. In all three letters from France, they tell me that you are such a good patient, and I am pleased to hear that, in spite of all that you have suffered.

Well dear, a week from tomorrow, Wyatt and Gústa will be confirmed, if nothing happens, and we will take communion. My three oldest will be far away, but none so far as you, my darling. I hope that it will not be so long until we will have you with us again.

I was so glad to see in the last minister's letter that you have not lost your faith in our Redeemer and Friend, for He is ever near us. Well my Dear, I will stop for the night as Papa is home and this is Saturday night and all the children in bed, sound asleep. Will continue tomorrow.

MAY 20TH.

Sunday morning, and a bright, warm day. No service today until 7:30 P.M. Then we all hope to be able to go to church, those that are home. Margrjét is at present in St. Andrews with Uncle John, but she is coming home this week.

Now my darling, you will be getting a lot of letters since we know your right address, and we all will keep writing. I only hope when Frank has seen you, he will write and tell us of your wounds. Dearest Archie, I think of your wounds at night, and in the morning I'm wondering how you have been able to rest at night. It does no good, but a mother's heart can't help it.

Poor Julli Stefansson's mother. Julli's name is among the missing and that must be so hard for her, the uncertainty and the waiting to hear more.

I am sending you a clipping about Steffans Sigurdson's death. He is to be buried on the 22nd in Hnausa. It seems a shock to a whole lot of people, but not to me.

Guðrún Steins was buried yesterday. Her two daughters were here. One of her grandsons was killed, and one wounded. Jón Pjeturson was killed, and Jóhann A. Pjeturson. It's pretty hard for them. Those boys are from Calgary, and their mother lives there.

Empire Day will be celebrated in the park, and on that day, you boys will be remembered here at any rate. Everybody that I meet, they all ask about you and when I expect you to come home, but that is one question that I cannot answer. Your father is going to write to you very soon, and you will get an interesting letter. I will try in the future to make my letters interesting.

My feelings at present are both rejoicing and anxious, that I am not in the mood to write as cheerful as I would like to be. You, my darling boy, perhaps will understand.

Papa has gone out for a walk this morning, and he is going as far as Mr. Bristow's, to tell him about our letters. They have the measles, and do not leave the house.

I hope that you will get the letters and snap shots that I sent to you. How about the money order that I sent to you in France? Did you get it yet, and if there is anything that you would like me to send to you? If so, then ask some-body to write it. All the children send their love, and Old Maggie. We are in the same house still, and Papa at Tergesen's working in the store and Florence at McLeod's Bakery. [McLeod's Bakery is referred to many times in Elisabet's letters but there is no record of its existence.]

Well dear, I must close. Oh, I pray for your speedy recovery, and that we get you soon back to us, my darling.

Your ever Loving mother
E. Th. Polson

Archie heard from Mrs. Tyler, whom he had visited before departing for France. He must have been lonely, because he asked Mrs. Tyler to visit him in Stockport, which is a long way from Somerset. Mrs. Tyler, for her part, writes that she is looking forward to Archie visiting her when he got sick leave. Mrs. Tyler mentions Pete Olson, as she has done in past correspondence, and laments that he did not come to visit them before going to France.

MAY 21ST

My dear Polson,

I was so pleased to get your letter today, and to hear that you're getting on well. If you could get me a railway pass, or a voucher as they call them for me, I would come and see you, if you would like me to do so. I don't know if they would grant me one, but as you have no relations in England to come to vis-it you they might do so in my case. You might ask, and perhaps they would pay one way, as it is a long way from here and in these days, it costs so much.

How nicely you write with your left arm and hand. I am so sorry that you have lost your right arm, but as you say, you are lucky to be alive. I have not heard from your mother, but will write to her again today and tell her that I have heard from you and that you are in England. I guess her letters to you have gone to France.

I am glad that your cousin came to see you. This is indeed a cruel war, and we at home can't imagine what you poor boys go through out there. We shall be *very pleased to see you when you get your sick leave. Are you able to get about? One of our men has been in hospital in Woolrich nearly six months. His wife, who works in our shop, has had three passes to go and see him.*

I sent your message to Margaret by her daddy today. Mick and all of his family are so pleased to hear news of you, and hope to see you soon. I am sorry Pete Olson did not come to see us before he left England.

The weather is nice. My sister is going to write to you. Let me know if there is anything that you want. With kind regards from Mr. Tyler, my love and our best wishes. Yours sincerely,

M.C. Tyler.

Constance Scott of the Red Cross wrote to Elísabet on May 22 with another positive report on his recovery.

INFORMATION BUREAU
CANADIAN RED CROSS SOCIETY,
14/16 COCKSPUR STREET,
LONDON S.W. 1.
22ND MAY, '17
IN ANSWERING PLEASE REPEAT NAME, NUMBER,
AND BATTALION OF SOLDIER.

Dear Madam
I BEG TO INFORM YOU THAT *Pte. J. Polson 721948 2nd M.G. Co.*
WHO IS NOW AT *Stepping Hill, Hospital, Stockport, Eng.*
has again been seen there by our authorised Red Cross visitor. I am glad to be able to tell you that she reports that he is doing very well. He is so bright & cheerful. He is a general favourite & makes many friends in the hospital.

Hoping that this good progress will continue.

Yours very truly
Constance Scott.
pp D.F.

Since Archie's arrival in England, the good news never seemed to stop. Elísabet received the second set of letters from Mrs. Paine and the Red

Cross and felt quite upbeat. She wrote to Archie on Whit Sunday, or Pentecost, which is celebrated on the seventh Sunday after Easter. Pentecost is a major religious festival for Icelandic Lutherans in Canada and in Iceland. Wyatt and Gústa had just been confirmed as members of the Lutheran Church. It was a great day for the family, though Elísabet was also thinking of her darling boy.

In the letter, refers to Josie Johanneson Búastaðum. This is one example of the ways the Icelanders dealt with the frequent name duplication. In this case, one Josie Johanneson is differentiated from another by the addition of the name of the farm where she lived.

GIMLI, MAY 27, 1917.

Dear Archie,

My Darling Boy,

Just a week tonight since I wrote to you, and sent it to England. Well, last night I got two most welcome letters from England, telling me how you were getting on, one from the Red Cross, and one from (Mrs.) Annie Paine. They're both telling me that you are getting better, but, of course, I know that it is a slow but sure recovery. That is how it seems to me.

Oh, my darling, what awful pain you must have when your wounds are dressed. Oh, how glad we are that it is possible for us to think and live in the hope that we will get you back to us again.

Well dear, this is Whit Sunday, and we are back home from church, and Gústa and Wyatt were confirmed. Your papa and Margrjét, Florence and I all took communion, and I thought of you, my darling, so far away and that you had done the same before leaving France. How glad that made me.

The church was full as usual. The church looked very nice, and this has been a splendid day for me all through. Papa is home here reading. The children went out for a walk with Noonie. Papa and I gave Gústa and Wyatt a hymn book each, and Arni and Petra gave each of them a dollar bill. Bill and Blythe gave Gústa a birthday ring, or rather a ring with her birthday stone in it.

Margrjét came home on the 24th of May, and Dorothy, Mr. and Mrs. Thorarinson and Rúna came down for the day. Margrjét is feeling much better now that she has had a good rest at Uncle's. Florence is working at McLeod's Bakery and I think that she likes it there. The weather keeps rather cold for this time of the year. The fishermen have not gone north yet, but expect they will go about the end of the week, or the beginning of next.

Last 24 of May, Josie Johanneson Búastaðum married this fellow of hers, I do not know his name. Rev. Carl Olson married them. I hope you got the letters with the snapshots in. I sent them to the hospital you are in.

Well, my darling, I must close as it is getting near mailing time. All the children are back again, and they send their love to you, as does Father. I hope by now that Frank has seen you, as it was in one of my letters that he had been sent for.

With heaps of love from your own loving mother.

E. Th. Polson.

Archie's letter of May 3 finally arrived, having been almost a month in transit, and Ágúst was motivated to write to his son in reply. He talks about the challenges of his working life, family life and what was going on in the Gimli of 1917. While the letter is dated June 3rd, he actually wrote it over several weeks. He encloses a copy of a letter from the Department of Militia and Defence dated June 8th and Elísabet refers to his writing a letter of her own to Archie dated June 17th.

Ágúst explains in colourful language the circumstances upon which he left s&t. He uses a sarcastic Icelandic expression, *Jóhannessar Söfnuð,* meaning 'Jóhannes' congregation' to describe their store in Gimli. He is referring to his former employer, Jóhannes Sigurdson, for whom he has little affection. s & t's premises in Gimli were located across the street from Tergesen's Store.

Snyder has found some temporary work. H.P. is opening a fruit stand and ice cream parlour in the back of the store, and has hired Snyder to decorate it. By this time Gimli has become a popular summer retreat for Winnipeg residents, so it is small wonder therefore that H.P would expand his operation in this way. Snyder did other work for H.P., in particular, he painted murals throughout H.P.'s house in Gimli that are still intact today.

The original letter is covered with ink blotches which greatly frustrates Ágúst. He blames Eaton's where the pen which was purchased. The T. Eaton Co. Limited was once Canada's largest department store retailer. The Eaton's mail order catalogue was a staple in rural and small town Canada, and therefore was a competitor of Tergesen's Store.

GIMLI, SUNDAY, JUNE 3RD, 1917.

My dear son Archie,

You cannot imagine how glad we all were to receive your long and welcome letter last Friday, and the writing was simply wonderful. I am sorry indeed that you should meet with this misfortune to lose your right arm, but we thank the Lord that He spared your life, and that we will see you again in the near future.

I don't really know what news to tell you, because Mother has written to you every week, although you have not got them. Why did I leave S & T? Well, I'll tell you. When old Joe sent me to that godforsaken place last summer [Riverton], I certainly gave him hell, and told him what I thought of him. It's a wonder that he didn't fire me there and then, but the old cuss wanted me out to the river so bad that he had to keep me on.

Of course, he told me that since I was so dissatisfied, that he would try to get me a good job in the City. He gave me a very good recommendation in Mirreck Anderson Co.[47] and others. And I think that I am sure of a job when I decide to go to Winnipeg, and it all depends on how things turn out when you come back.

H.P. wanted me too, and I decided to try him, as I am not very fond of changing places. I have been there just two months. I wanted to see if I help him to pull through a bit. I would like to buck Jóhannessar Söfnuð on the corner a bit.

Mother, Margrjét, Gústa and Wyatt went to the Peg [Winnipeg] this morning. Margrjét is to be examined by a specialist, Dr. Jón Stefanson, who has been treating her throughout. She might have consumption. Mother called me up today, saying that Margrjét was okay as far as consumption, but Dr. Stefanson is going to treat her for throat trouble. They will be home tomorrow.

Well son, this is getting to be quite a place for autos. Jón Einarsson and Dori Pjeturson have a new Ford. Thor Lifman, Geo. [illegible], Baldi Anderson and Myers have one each.

Mrs. Dalman was in the store today. She showed me a letter from Arthur. He was asking her for your address. He said that he was going to try to look you up. I guess that it will be a long time till you two meet.

Well, I think I'll finish this letter tonight. It's been two weeks since I started it.

We had nine of our children for supper last evening because Bonnie came down on the four o'clock train, and left on the 7:40, and mother is telling you about Josie being here. I bought the little house with the screens around it from Jón Einarson, and had it moved down here for the girls to sleep in. Then I bought a wardrobe from Bill McLeod to put in it so they have a small place of their own. We got a letter from Ottawa about you. We send you a copy of it herewith.

I had just sent you a box of stuff, the very same day that we got your letter. I didn't put any tobacco in it, as I didn't think that you were allowed to smoke. According to your letter, such is not the case.

A week ago last Saturday, I sent you another one weighing 4 ½ lbs., all tobacco. I hope that you have it by the time that you get this letter. I bought "express delivery", so that you would get it without delay.

We got a letter from the Red Cross headquarters in London, saying that you are getting along fine, and that you are a general favourite in the hospital, and making many friends. Florence Jónasson is working for us. Tergesen partitioned the store off, and has a fruit stand and ice cream parlour in the back.

He got Snyder to decorate it. Tergesen got a letter from Pete a week ago, and he said that he was going to see you, and, of course, he has been there by this time. This is a hell of a pen to write with, but what can you expect? It was bought at Eaton's.

Well, we are getting to be quite a farm. We have a cow, a heifer, one hen, nine chickens, six turkeys, six pigeons, one sheep, one dog and two cats, but no horse. I think that I told you about what happened to poor Blackie last winter.

Now son, if there's anything you want your old dad to send to you, just let me know, and I'll endeavor to get it to you. Should you want five dollars, *mention it and the best way to send it. Mother wrote to Mrs. Tyler, and sent her some snapshots of the sheep and the kids. Whenever you come, you wire us from Ottawa or some place in Canada, so that we can meet you in the Peg.*

The Government in Ottawa are going to put on conscription. They want a hundred thousand men. With some of the shirkers here all shaking in their boots, the poor devils.

It appears that all the boys from here are okay so far, but poor Lully. Ingi has written several letters, but I don't think he likes it any too well.

Well my boy, I think that I'll close this time. Will write again soon.

Good to be with you.

Your loving Dad, A.G. Polson

Mrs. Tyler wrote to Archie again, and reiterated her invitation for a visit.

JUNE 7TH

Dear Archie,

Hope you are getting on well. I had a nice letter from your mother today, and she asked me to send on the enclosed to you. When do you think that you will be able to leave long enough to visit?

I am just catching the train to go over to Merton for the afternoon, so excuse a short note. Will you send me Pete Olson's address, if you know it? He has sent three cards the last two weeks, and I should like to write and to send him something.

This awful war seems as bad as ever. The weather is lovely now, and the farmers will soon be starting haymaking.

I hope that you will be able to come to us during the summer, either July, August or early in September, while the weather is nice. Our kind regards, and best wishes.

M.C. Tyler.

By letter dated June 8, 1917, almost exactly two months after Archie was wounded, the military sent its first correspondence since the Night Lettergrams early in April. It was a formal confirmation from the Director of Records that Archie was wounded. The letter was written with a cold formality. Archie wrote in his letter started on May 3, 1917 that he was wounded when a German shell burst beside him. The Military now told his parents that "the marginally noted soldier" suffered gunshot wounds in the thigh and right arm "necessitating amputation of the latter."

DEPARTMENT OF MILITIA AND DEFENCE
OTTAWA, JUNE 8TH, 1917.
FROM: THE ADJUTANT-GENERAL
CANADIAN MILITIA.
TO: AGUST POLSON, ESQ.,
GIMIL, MANITOBA.
721948 PTE. ARCHIBALD JOHN POLSON,
CANADIAN EXPEDITIONARY FORCE.

Sir,

I have the honour to state that information has been received by mail from England, to the effect that the marginally noted soldier was admitted to the 2nd Western General Hospital, Manchester, England, on April 28th, 1917, suffering from gun shot wounds in the thigh and right arm, necessitating amputation of the latter.

2. Any further information received will be communicated to you without delay.

I have the honour to be,
Sir,
Your obedient servant,
[illegible] *Beard*
Director of Records
for a/Adjutant-General.

But the news from the Red Cross was still positive. Elísabet received three favourable reports in a row during the month of June, although the third report, dated June 16, included the comment that "he looks very weak".

INFORMATION BUREAU.
CANADIAN RED CROSS SOCIETY,
14/16 COCKSPUR STREET,
LONDON S.W. 1.
11.6.17.
IN ANSWERING PLEASE REPEAT NAME, NUMBER,
AND BATTALION OF SOLDIER.

Dear Madam,

I BEG TO INFORM YOU THAT Pte. J. Polson No. 721,948 2nd M.G. Co.
WHO IS NOW AT The Stepping Hill Hospital, Stockport, Cheshire, England
has again been seen there by our Representative, who reports that the patient
is very much better & is now able to go out.

Hoping that he will continue to make satisfactory progress.

Yours very truly,
Constance Scott
Per [illegible]

CANADIAN RED CROSS SOCIETY,
14/16 COCKSPUR STREET,
LONDON S.W. 1.
INFORMATION BUREAU.
20.6.17

Dear Madam

I BEG TO INFORM YOU THAT Pte. J. Polson No. 721948 2nd M.G. Co.
WHO IS NOW AT Stepping Hill, Hospital Stockport, Cheshire, England
was again recently visited by our authorised representative who tells us that
she found that he was doing well at the time of her visit.

We hope that this good progress may continue & that he may make a
good recovery.

Yours truly,
Constance Scott.

pp SWG

INFORMATION BUREAU.
CANADIAN RED CROSS SOCIETY,
14/16 COCKSPUR STREET,
LONDON S.W. 1.
26.6.17
IN ANSWERING PLEASE REPEAT NAME, NUMBER,
AND BATTALION OF SOLDIER.

Dear Madam

I BEG TO INFORM YOU THAT *Pte. J. Polson No. 721948 2nd M.G. Co. Can.* WHO IS NOW AT *The Stepping Hill Hospital Stockport, Cheshire, England, Has again been seen by our visitor who reports that he is improving, and is able to be out a great deal; though as is to be expected, he looks very weak, hoping that he will continue to make steady progress, I am yours very truly,*

Constance Scott.
Per DCK.

Elísabet tried to write to Archie at least once a week, bringing him up to date on the local news. Once again she writes in Icelandic. Archie was never far from her thoughts.

GIMLI JUNE 17, 1917
My dearest Archie,
You see that this is Sunday again and I am writing. Frank Ward went home last Monday morning and it rained cats and dogs. We have had lots of rain, and the farmers are all rejoicing. But now we want the warm weather to get the full benefit of it. Josie and Jean are here and feel fine. Uncle Snyder came down last night and we were all here for dinner. There was Jóhann, Jean, Noonie, Snyder and our family. So our table was full. We like a houseful, or at least I like a houseful of our friends. Bonnie stayed until 7:40, so we all had supper together. We wanted you to be with us to make it complete, but we will soon have you, we hope.

Last week was a busy one for me. There was a Home Economic Society meeting organized this spring, and I was elected president. This week they sent a nurse down to demonstrate, and I had to be there every afternoon. Our meetings are conducted in English. We have one meeting each month, and then I have my Ladies Aid meeting to attend, and we try to do a little Red Cross work on the side. We are fine so far, but I expect your sister will not be fine all July.

Now the weather is getting better, but it is not hot yet. There were a lot of the vacationers leaving, but that was before the summer weather. Many have left, but many come when school is out. [Jóhannes] Sigurdson came down here last Friday.

There's lots of talk about Conscription, but I can't tell whether anything will happen. It has been threatened so often before. I believe that some of the boys are shaking with fear, thinking about it.

Gústi Magnússon has the restaurant, but I have never been in there. I haven't been getting around much, and therefore I don't hear much news. Björn Ólson has been at the General Hospital for a long time. He had an operation from an old hernia, but is expected home this week.

Now the school is almost over, finished on the 22nd and the Sunday School Picnic is on the 23rd, this coming Saturday.

The measles are infesting here and Josie is afraid that Jean will get it. Jean and Josie are sending you a big box. I got a letter from Mrs. Tyler last week, and she had then just got the letter from you. She wrote such a nice letter.

How do you like the English language over there at the hospital? I can't start counting everybody that sends you their greetings, but here are some I have seen lately and everybody asks about you. Then it is, Magga á Bakkanum, Margrjét Karvelson, cousin Anna, Jón and Thórður, Sigurbjörg and Karin, Petra and Árni's sister Mrs. Guðmundsson, Snæbjörn Mooncy, Jóhanna and also everyone here, all the siblings and old Maggie, she has not forgotten you, old cousin Björg and cousin Ingibjörg. I think I will stop here because I can see that your father is writing you a long letter. That pleases me very much. He has been so good, and I hope God will reward him for that.

Well my dearest, I hope God will give you speedy recovery and guide you home to us again.

Your loving mother,
E. Th. Polson

Archie's younger siblings took great pleasure in writing to their big brother. Here is a sampling from fourteen-year-old Wyatt.

GIMLI, MANITOBA
JUNE 18, 1917
Dear Archie,

It is quite a while since we got a letter from you. We have six young turkeys and nine young chickens. I own the chickens. The cow has been sick all winter, but she is getting better now. We have not been driving her to the pasture yet, as we got permission to have her in the town while she was sick. But we will soon be putting her in the pasture as usual.

School will be over, and then we will have lots of fun when it is over. I am planning to go out to Uncle John's when school is over. I have a standing invitation to come to see him this summer.

I have not gone out bathing yet, but a lot of the other boys have. They say that it is pretty cold yet. We have been having rain for the last week. The sun shines once in a few days. We all got into our heads to write to you and keep you busy reading. I have not heard of Mundi for nearly a month so I think that he is well, and is so interested in the war that he doesn't find time to write. I guess he is busy killing Germans. Konnie is doing some arithmetic.

I can't find any more news to tell you, so goodbye.

Your loving brother,
Wyatt Polson.

P.S Everybody is saying how well you write with your left arm. Many thanks for the letter you wrote just before you were wounded. W.P.

Josie was staying with the Polsons in Gimli while she awaited the birth of her child. She added a further postscript to Wyatt's letter.

20/6/17
Letter dated May 24th was recently received from Mundi. He has been in France for some time, but seen no trench life as yet.

Josie Ward.

A few days later, Elísabet wrote to Archie, starting in Icelandic, switching to English and then back to Icelandic. Among other things, she reports on news that she had just received about Mundi and also about Frank. This is the last we hear of Mundi in the letters. Mundi would serve on the front lines for eighteen months and participated in the battles at Hill 70 and Passchendaele. He escaped the war without physical injury but was debilitated for the rest of his life by what we now know as post-traumatic stress disorder. Mundi returned home in February of 1919. He never married and died in 1951. Mundi remained a close friend of the Polsons.

Jóhannes Sigurdson's wife has been asking about Archie. Jóhannes and his family moved to Winnipeg in 1911, although he retained his interest in the S & T's stores. They kept a summer home in Gimli. It is not known whether Archie ever wrote to Jóhannes as he had suggested in his last letter before leaving for France.

Elísabet mentions Húsavík, a small fishing community located about 8 kilometers south of Gimli. Like many of the place names in New Iceland, Húsavík is named after a town in Iceland, in this case, a fishing village in the north of Iceland.

GIMLI JUNE 24, 1917

My dearest, dearest boy,

How we look forward to the time when we get to see you, and have you at home with us again—and not just us but many, many others. I trust that God will grant you recovery, and lead you successfully home to us.

Yesterday I got a letter from my Bonnie, and she said that now our blessed Frank is over in France. I will pray to God Almighty to protect him and keep him safe from all the danger that awaits him, and I hope and know that you will help me pray to God to give him back to his mother, and to all of us.

I certainly feel for her, even if she remains strong because what else can be done? We must be ungrudging, whatever comes our way.

I got a letter from Mrs. Tyler. I don't remember if I mentioned that to you. In the letter she said that she can't see you because you are so far away, but you will come to her when you will be well, and that makes me feel better.

Pete Tergesen has written home and said he will go and see you as soon as he gets the address. He is in Shorncliffe.

The Sigurdson family came down last Friday, and yesterday Mrs. Sigurdson stopped me on the street to ask about you and about your letter that you wrote yourself. Yesterday, our Sunday School picnic was held in the park and we had a very nice time. Last night was the first dance of the season in the park. The girls, Florence and Margrjét, went with Daniel after Florence stopped working, and when they came home afterwards, we all had coffee and then to bed.

Margaret and Sigga Páls were our banner bearers as we had no boys big enough. There were enough boys when we got out to the park and they served refreshments at the picnic. We had, as I said before, a lovely time, although we did not go until 2 o'clock in the afternoon. There is quite a crowd of people down for the summer, but I won't name them all.

Now school is closed for the summer. Wyatt passed in to Grade VII, Lena to Grade V, Fjóla to Senior III and Bonnie Class 13. Gústa is in Grade VIII, but did not take exams as she did not return to school after confirmation.

(The cow has arrived so I must go out and do the milking and Maggie is yelling, "The cow is here Mrs. Polson.")

Well I have finished milking and fed the calf, and now the milk is being delivered and I have forgotten so much I wanted to say.

Einar, Mundi´s brother, got a letter from Mundi from France written May 24th. He has been there a month and has not been in the front line, but expected to be there soon.

Your Aunt Rúna has poisoning in [her] lip but was better when I heard last. Papa was home all day working at his books but is just gone out for a walk. We had no service today as the Minister confirmed at Húsavík today.

Maggie has just gone home and she sends her best regards to you. She is wearing the hat you bought for her two years ago. Everybody sends their love to you from here, and you know how many that is. It would take a whole page

to write them all. I am sending this week Gústa and Wyatt's pictures. God
bless you my dearest.

Your loving mother
E. Th. Polson

Elísabet wrote to Archie on Dominion Day, once again in Icelandic. She
tells him that Stjana Orr is a "different girl from when he knew her".
Once again she buries this disclosure amid a flurry of gossip in an effort
to lessen its impact. So it looks like at some point Archie must have have
received a "Dear John" letter, which would explain why none of the correspondence with Stjana has survived.

GIMLI MAN. BOX 84
JULY 1, 1917
My dearest Archie,
Again I sit down to write you a few lines to let you know that we are still think-
ing of you and often. I can't say that the heat is bothering us. We have not real-
ly had one completely hot day. It is just good working weather.

   It pleased me very much that I got a letter from The Red Cross, and it said
that you are getting better and you are moving around. How is the wound on
your thigh, and can you step on that foot? I have not heard much about your
wounds, but everybody is asking me about them and when you will be coming home to us.

   We are all in good health. Josie and Frank are here with us, there is still
plenty of room for you, my dearest boy, when you come. I know that your father
is looking so much forward to your homecoming, and I know that you understand how much I look forward to it, my dearest.

   Frank Ward came last Friday and goes back tomorrow morning, so this
is not much rest for him. Frank talks often about you, my dear. I wish you
could be here and hear them talk about you. (You would feel quite pleased.)

   Well, it will soon be supper time and I will have to be getting supper
ready. Papa and Frank walked downtown and have just got back. They say
that the town is dead, but the train to Winnipeg was crowded last night.

[Elísabet took a break for supper.] Well, supper is over now, and I'm through milking, so here I am again and there is a west wind. The creek is flooded but the water does not run over the sidewalk. We hope it will be down in the morning.

Well, yesterday Margrjét started working at Tergesen's store. She is going to try it and see whether she can stand it. I hope that she can, as it will help some. I have not been any place this week except to the wedding that Papa is telling you about. It seems Stjana is a different girl from what she was when you knew her, but I may be mistaken. Nobody may think this but me and you know how odd I am.

Frank is playing on an old mouth organ of yours just now. We hope to get a letter from you this week. Have you got any parcels yet from us? Tell us in your next letter, and how to send you money when you need it. I am sure that Papa will send you some as soon as he knows how he should send it. Well, my darling, ask for the things you want and we will try and get them for you as soon as we know more. I will be sending a box soon. Everybody is asking about you, and sending their love.

Your Loving mother,
E. Th. Polson

Eleven-year-old Lena decided to send a letter to Archie as well. Elísabet must have enclosed it with her letter.

JULY 1ST
1917
Dear Archie,
Mother, Father and Florence are writing you. So I said to myself, I might as well write Archie. This is not very good writing. Jean Ward is just saying good-night. Jean always says good-night to everyone. I think you'd be glad to stop school if you were me. I guess you know who Jean is? It is Josies [sic] sister daughter, Leona Jean Ward [the daughter of Josie's sister-in-law]. She is at our place now, and Josie and Frank. I am so very glad that our school need not start school till September. I guess I am telling you the same news as

the ones that are writing you. Gústa is writing you too. I think I had better close. Your loving sister.

Lena Polson

P.S. I will write you later about 4 pages. I turned my name around and it was Anel Noslop
Lena Polson

Elísabet wrote to Archie again on July 8. The letter was written in Icelandic, with a postscript in English. While Archie had apparently written to others, he had not bothered to write to his mother since early May. Elísabet is desperate to hear from him and begs him to write. There is some good news; the owner of their house has agreed to let them stay on as renters.

Elísabet mentions that Hannes Pálmason has been helping Ágúst with "working the books". Ágúst's was the local property assessor, and the books likely related to that work. Also, Ágúst and Elísabet attended a party at Jóhannes Sigurdsson's home. Elísabet writes that they had a good time. One suspects that Ágúst had a different opinion.

Elísabet makes a wry comment about Professor Skúli Johnson, and his loss of the lovely Ásta. She suggests that perhaps he should find an English girl "if the Icelandic girls aren't good enough." Professor Johnson became a renowned professor of Classics.[48] In 1921, he married a girl who was born in Northern Ireland.

GIMLI JULY 8, 1917
My dear Archie,
It's Sunday but there was no service because we had no priest, but one is to come soon. I wrote to you last Sunday, the first of July, but Dominion Day was celebrated on Monday. Nobody came to see me from Winnipeg, and all was very quiet.

On Tuesday and Wednesday I worked in the garden with Jonson, and on Thursday I went to the Home Economics Society meeting. On Friday I did the washing, and yesterday I did all the cleaning and then went with Gústa,

Dorothy [Frank Polson's sister], Wyatt, Fjóla, and Konráð to the movies, but Lena had already seen it before. Dorothy came yesterday on the 4:00 train and is staying with us.

Margrjét is working at Tergesen's and was so busy yesterday that when I came back from the movies, I went to help her wash glasses and ice cream dishes. Mrs. Tergesen was also there helping. Then we went home because Florence was finished working at McLeod's.

All day your father has been with Hannes Pálmason working the books. I don't know when they will be done. Pálmason is doing this so that your father doesn't have to miss a day at the store.

It is much more busy at Tergesen's than it was last year at this time, but I don't know how it's going for Sigurdson's. Olöf Johnson works there as a principal and Thórður Jóhannes Freeman, Jóhannes Christie and Jóhannes Sigurdson himself. I think that all the stores are doing good business right now, but so far there are not as many of our people around as there were last year. I heard that Professor Skúli Johnson is here now. I saw him from a distance. I think that he is feeling better after losing his girlfriend. That is good. Ásta is beautiful, but there are more around. Maybe an English girl, if the Icelandic girls aren't good enough.

Jón Thorðarson is here on his holiday at my brother Jón's. He came last Wednesday.

Mrs. Erlindson, who owns this house, came from the south last week with her children. She wants to stay in Gimli, but she wants to continue renting the house to us, and she is looking for a little place for herself. She said that my people are doing well.

I forgot to mention that your father and I were invited to a party at Jóhannes Sigurdson's home on Monday evening and we had a good time. I hope your father tells you about it.

My dear Archie, I would appreciate it so much if you would send me just a few lines. I know that it is difficult for you to write, but we long to see something, a note from you, if it's possible. We would like to know if you have got any of the parcels which we have sent. And if you are short of anything or need us to send you some money, we could send it to Mrs. Tyler. Do you have any *idea when you will get better so you can start the journey home to us? We are told that all the Canadian men get their discharge in Toronto.*

Konnie is standing beside me and is asking countless questions about you. Josie is lying down in the hammock, and Jean and Margrjét are working today like other days. Florence and Dorothy and Gústa are playing on the lawn, and Lena and Fjóla have gone to McLeod's Bakery. Maggie is setting the table for supper.

I can't remember the number of people who have asked about you and when you are coming home. We are living with the hope that we get you home to us, my dear. I heard yesterday that Ralph Malcolm will be home again soon. He's being discharged because of his lungs.

Aunt Nina has been sick but is better now.

God be with you, my dear, to bless you and guide you and send you safely home to us.

Your loving mother,
E.Th. Polson

P.S. Dear Archie,
I hope that you will be getting on as well as possible, and you will help all you can to get better. Give my love to the kind hearts who are nursing you my darling boy.

From your own loving mother,
E. Th. Polson.

On July 15, Elísabet wrote a touching note to Archie.

GIMLI JULY 15 1917
My Dear Archie,
I am just letting you see that I remember you my dear son although I have had lots to do and little sleep because during the night Josie gave birth to a boy on the hour.

Your loving mother, E. Th. Polson

Bonnie apparently wrote often, but only two of her letters were found among Archie's papers. The following is one of them. Bonnie seems to be doing a little matchmaking, promoting a young woman named Lolla, We do not know which Lolla this may be, because at least three Lollas wrote to Archie while he was overseas.

Snyder has found yet another job. He will be employed by Ruddy Kester (not Rudy Koester) which would later years merge with Claude Neon and dominate Winnipeg's outdoor signage business for many years.

WINNIPEG, MANITOBA
NURSES HOME
JULY 20, 1917.

Dearest Archie,

You must be having a gay time these days in the sunshine. I suppose that you go out a lot. We don't know much, my dear, as we haven't heard from you for such a long time, but we are hoping to have you with us before very long. Are our hopes too farfetched, do you think?

You remember the Mr. Bruce that I've been telling you about, that star patient of mine, and how interested he was in you. Well, he wants to give you a job, or did I tell you this before? Anyway, I'll tell it again. It's as junior inspector of concrete roads, or something.

It's nice to have a job of some sort to look forward to. I think that it was awfully nice of him to think of it. Don't you think so? I showed him a picture of you, and he liked your face. Everyone likes your face, except me, of course. (Actually, I think that you're A-1, though you might not have known it, my big soldier brother.)

Emma is back from holidays. Her holidays are over. She had a good time and liked Gimli awfully well, not just the Polsons, and the Polsons were greatly taken with her.

I am to have my holidays in August. These have been stifling days, and our clothes just stick to us lately, and the patients suffer greatly with the heat. It is a lot cooler today. Thank goodness.

I have had two letters from Frank, but no news or anything of interest in them, except that I need not worry about you as you will be alright, and that we will soon have you back. Have you heard from Frank at all?

Have your heard our nephew's name? Frank Archibald Edward Ward. Now isn't that something like a name? I would have been awfully disappointed had they not given him your name.

Everyone says that he's the dearest thing, and, of course, I know that he is, without being told. Have you heard from Lolla lately? She took first class honours in her music exam this year. Smart girl.

I hear that she's engaged, but don't think that it's true for she would have told me. It seems that everyone is getting engaged or married. Let them hop to it, says I. It's not worrying me a great deal.

Uncle Snyder is still working up here. He is painting for an advertising firm now, the Rudy Koester Agency. He is making good money on it too.

Well, Darling, this will have to suffice for the time. I wish that you'd try to pen me just a few lines.

Goodbye, dear boy,
Lovingly,
Bonnie.

For some reason, there were no further letters home from Archie and yet we know that he wrote to others. The reason for this neglect may be that writing letters was an onerous task, and Archie believed he would be seeing his family soon anyway. The family did continue to receive favourable reports on his recovery. The Red Cross report of July 17, 1917 was the most positive yet. For some reason, this letter was signed on behalf of E. Bovey, rather than Ms. Scott.

CANADIAN RED CROSS SOCIETY,
14/16 COCKSPUR STREET,
LONDON S.W. 1.
INFORMATION BUREAU.
17th July 1917

Dear Madam,

I BEG TO INFORM YOU THAT *Pte. J. Polson No. 721,948 2nd* M.G. Co. WHO IS NOW AT THE *Stepping Hill Hospital, Stockport, Cheshire, England.*

has been visited by our authorised representative three times since I last wrote to you. Each report about him says that he not only looks, but is much stronger, and that he is very happy and almost always out of doors.

Yours truly,
E. Bovey. pp [illegible]

Around this time, Archie heard again from Josie. One can imagine Archie shaking his head as he read the first part of this post card.

GIMLI, MAN.
JULY 18TH/17
Your little nephew "Frank" is peacefully sleeping, but will take your place in the army as soon as he is big enough to shoulder his gun. From Florence's letter you will have learned that he arrived on the 15th. He has lots of black hair, large blue eyes, quite prominent features—and is very good.

Daddy came yesterday, and left this morning. They are busily haying. Bill just got back from the jury duty on Monday. Pat is helping. Haying is very late this year. If roads and weather are favourable, Bob and Frank will come in their car on Saturday.

We are hoping for further news from you, and of you.

Heaps of love from Frank, Jean and Josie

On July 19, Archie was transferred to Granville Canadian Special Hospital –known as Chatham House Hospital–in Ramsgate, along the English Channel. A month later, the federal Director of Records wrote to the Polsons. It was only the second communication they received from the Military since the two Night Lettergrams. It seems to have been written from the same unfortunate template as the Director's earlier letter, and advised of his transfer to Ramsgate. This time the writer correctly writes that "the soldier marginally noted" suffered shrapnel wounds to his thigh, but then mistakenly refers to his left arm also being injured, "necessitating amputation." It was, of course, Archie's right arm.

DEPARTMENT OF MILITIA AND DEFENCE
OTTAWA, AUGUST 21ST, 1917.
FROM: THE ADJUTANT-GENERAL
CANADIAN MILITIA.
TO: AGUST POLSON, ESQ.,
GIMLI, MAN.
721948 PTE. ARCHIBALD JOHN POLSON,
CANADIAN EXPEDITIONARY FORCE.

Sir,

I have the honour to state that information has been received by mail from England, to the effect that the soldier marginally noted was transferred from the Second Western General Hospital, Manchester, England, to the Granville Canadian Special Hospital, Ramsgate, England on July 19th, 1917, suffering from shrapnel wounds in the thigh and left arm, necessitating amputation of the left arm.

2. Any further information received will be communicated to you without delay.

I have the honour to be,

Sir,

Your obedient servant,

[illegible] *Beard*

Director of Records

for a/Adjutant-General.

Elísabet wrote to Archie again on July 22. One can imagine that she must have been desperate to receive a second letter from Archie, but she tries not to let on.

GIMLI, JULY 22ND, 1917

Dearest Archie,

My Darling Boy,

It seems so long since I have heard from you, and it seems so long since I have written. It is two weeks today since I have written you. Florence wrote last Sunday as I had lost so much sleep on account of little Frankie arriving that morning (that is what we call Josie's baby). Josie and baby are both fine. Frank

Ward came last Tuesday and went the next morning. Yesterday, Frank came with Bob Neal and old Mr. Ward in Bob Neal's car, and they left again in the afternoon, at 3 o'clock. Wyatt went with them for a short stay, and was in his glory. What do you think Josie's baby is to be called? It is to be named nothing less than Frank Archibald Edward Ward. How is that for a high? Baby is a nice little fellow, and so good, like his Uncle Archie.

My Darling, I will not be able to write much news as my time is short, but hope to write more this week. We are all fine here, and hope that you are getting stronger, my darling. We have only had the one letter from you, but hope to hear from you soon. Everybody sends their love.

Your ever loving mother,
E. Th. Polson

Archie's convalescence went well, and he started to plan for the future. While the government tried as much as possible to return soldiers to their previous occupations, they did in the case of disabled soldiers offer a certain amount of retraining.[49]

It appears that, as always, Archie was looking on the bright side, and anticipated the opportunity to get an education that he or his family could not have otherwise afforded. His sister, Florence, later wrote:

The secretary of the Municipality of Gimli offered Archie his position when he heard that he had lost his arm. Archie was grateful, but he said that he would be going to Normal School and would teach. He said, 'I hope I will make a good teacher.'

After his move to Ramsgate, Archie once again wrote to Mrs. Tyler. He was now much closer to her home in Somerset. Mrs. Tyler replied.

JULY 26TH
Dear Polson,
Many thanks for your letter. We are so pleased to hear that you have been moved to a Canadian Convalescent Home. I hope that you won't get any raids

while you are at Ramsgate. You are certainly seeing some of this country while you are here.

We shall be very pleased to see you when you get leave, but I hope that you get longer than six days sick leave. I am sure that you are anxious and looking forward to going back to Canada to see all your people. How pleased your mother and all will be to see you again. I thought that you would have had your artificial arm fitted in England. Burnham [a resort town located near Highbridge] is very full right now with visitors. I hope that you will get your leave while the weather is nice, and the days long.

Margaret is here. [Presumably Margaret was a friend or relative who Archie met on his first visit.] She has a broken bone in her arm. She fell off her bike at her home ten days ago. She has been here a week. I am expecting two of my sisters August 1st for their holiday.

I hope that you'll be able to get Pete Olson's address. This awful war seems as bad as ever. How well you write with your left arm. With kind regards and best wishes, and hoping to see you soon.

Yours sincerely,
M.C. Tyler

Archie received a couple of letters from his fellow soldiers. The first was a letter from a pal, Bill Goodman, a fellow Icelander.

This letter has the easy casualness of a discussion between long-time friends. Bill was in training in England, and he enclosed a "snap", meaning a photograph, of Bonnie and two other young women, all in nurses' uniforms. The photograph was given to Bill by Konnie Jóhanneson, whose sister was in training with Bonnie.

After the war, Konnie Jóhanneson gained renown as a member of the Winnipeg Falcons, a hockey team from the West End of Winnipeg, made up almost entirely of Icelandic war veterans. In 1920, the Falcons won the first hockey gold medal ever awarded, at the Antwerp Olympics.

294023 PTE. WM. GOODMAN.
E. CO.
11TH RESERVE BATTALION C.E.F.
SHORNCLIFFE, ENGLAND.

Dear Archie,

Well Archie, cut out swearing at me for here is the letter. You see, I lost the letter that you wrote on July 23rd, and as I could not find it anywhere, I decided that the only thing that I could do was wait until you wrote again, but now I found it in my fatigue pants, and will endeavor to answer it.

I met one of the Hermanson boys here. He is from Selkirk, from the 78th. He had been wounded.

In case the letter from me enclosing Art's address don't [sic] get to you, her is ir, Pte. Arthur Dalman, 622321, 44th Batt. BEF 10th Infantry Brig 4 Canadian Division France. I have not heard from him lately.

I hope that you have had your medical board, and are leaving for God's country soon, if not sooner. If you get to go Canada, never mind your leave here. Get there! Do you get me?

Well Archie, I would very much like to see you, but you must be here a year after you have had your leave till you get another. So for Heaven sake, try to come around here.

Say, I just found out that Pete Tergesen was in the gang that went to France shortly after we got here. I don't know his number, but will try to get his full address for you.

I will go around and see Skaptason next Sunday and see if he can give [me], or get me, your cousin's address.

We are now in the ten-week training program so how near I am to France taking first aid and machine gun. The instructor pulled a M.G. [machine gun] apart, and asked for the best mechanic in the class. Then the boys for a joke hollered "Bill!" He told me to put it together. Now I never saw a machine gun before, but I got her together.

Say Archie, I have a snap here that I am going to enclose. If you have any yourself, please send me one. You see, I never leave Camp, so I have no news. All's well at both home and in Gimli.

I expect to be an uncle of another boy or girl in a month. At least they expect Lena, who is married to Baldy [Short for Baldur] to have another. She has a girl already. I suppose that you know that.

Well Archie, I suppose you will have found it hard to figure this letter out, so I close with best regards, and hoping to hear from you in the near future.

Your old friend,
Bill.

A comical postcard was found among Archie's correspondence. It portrays a young boy dressed as soldier and carrying a toy rifle. The text reads: "I'm gonna be a soldier when I grow up. Some get shot, but more of 'em get half shot." The card was addressed to Archie's friend, Bill Goodman, at 688 Victor Street in the West End of Winnipeg which suggests that Bill had been wounded and sent home.

The letters from home became more and more mundane as Archie's expected return drew near. Elísabet wrote to Archie on August 5, and her letter was little more than a commentary on the comings and goings of the family. Part way through, Ágúst took over the writing. It was the calm before the storm.

Elísabet mentions that a fellow stayed at Loni. Loni Beach was, and is, a seasonal cottage community located just north of the Town of Gimli.

GIMLI, MAN.
AUG. 5, 1917
My Darling Boy,
I am writing a few lines again this Sunday because I have been so busy. I have often wished to write you in the week time, but not find time so far. Dorothy left last Sunday morning but Nina came down last night and will stay this week. Josie is here yet, but expects to go home a week from tomorrow. She is going to have the baby christened before she goes home. Bonnie has not had her holidays yet, but wants to have them before Josie goes with the children. Wyatt is still out at Erinview, but is coming home next Saturday with Frank Ward.

Your father, Josie, Nina and myself were asked to McLeod's for dinner and afternoon coffee, and now we are going over again to have supper there. I came home to write your letter and then Snæbjörn was waiting for us at home. He came down last night and is going back in the morning. He told us that Anna Thorvaldson has married Hlöðver Ágúst Arnason. You must know him because he was here at Gimli for some time with Einar Westman, but the last time he stayed at Loni and nobody seemed to know about it. She [Anna] phoned the news home Monday, and her father was not at home but her mother came to the phone. It has been a surprise.

Florence and Margrjét are working and Gústa is going out to Erinview with Josie. I see Papa coming for me to go for supper.

[At this point, Ágúst takes over.]

Mother went out to milk the cow. Then away we go to supper at McLeod's. Well old boy, I hope that you will be home soon, or at least we hear from you. I have worn out all your clothes, so we will have to knock someone down for a new suit of clothes when you get back.

I guess that mother has told you all the news, so what can I do? I take orders at the beach three times a week, and get a lot of my old customers such as Mrs. Paul (she has paid us over $85.00) and Mrs. Dr. White [sic], the young J. Reid, two Sharpes, [illegible] Munn, McRea, and a lot of new ones.

Our old customers are all the time asking about you. It takes me about an hour to tell them about you each day. We were very busy yesterday. I think that it is a long time since Tergi has seen such days as he has seen this summer.

I don't know what old Joe [his former employer, Jóhannes Sigurdson] will do about work this fall when Thorstein leaves. He only has the three of them now.

Here comes mother. She will have to put the finishing touch to this. There is great talk about conscription. The bill will pass the Senate this week, but we will have an election this fall, maybe late in September. You should be back by that time as you are on the voters' list.

[Elísabet returns from the barn and signs the letter.]

Lovingly your mother,
E. Th. Polson.

A soldier we know only as Jack had been a patient in Stockport when Archie was recuperating there. He wrote this lively letter in reply to one from Archie.

MONDAY
AUG. 6TH.
Dear Arch,

You will wonder why I have not answered your letter before this, but you will have to excuse me this time for I have been operated on again and I have just got out of bed. They cut all of the scar out and also a nerve over the end of the bone. I bleed quite a lot, and I still feel punk. Also caught a peach of a cold while I was in bed.

A few more Canucks arrived, and altogether there are over sixty patients here now. Most of the old bunch of nurses have gone to the work house. I had a short talk with Liddy the other day. All the girls send their regards also. Of course, Marion and Lizzie, and theirs.

Marion had her holidays the other week, and only the two of us went out on sort of a picnic, and I sure had a time. I have been out with her again since, and I sure had a whale of a time, if you know what I mean. I hardly did that, you know, but "by heck" it was a near thing.

I would just like to have a talk with you. Lizzie was telling Marion that "she wasn't in love with me," but Lord, Lizzie is jealous. She has been awful lately.

I got a one pound note from the pay office, and you should see the balance in my book, only about $106.31. I will tell them to wake up and figure it out again.

Well, how do you like Ramsgate now? And say, do our cases go to the hospital that you are in? I think it's pretty rotten to have the grub thrown at you like that. Do you manage other ways alright? Well, old son, guess this is all for this time, for I still feel shaky. Hope you are okay.

Yours till Hell freezes,
Jack.

At the end of August, Archie finally made his second visit to Mrs. Tyler and her family in Highbridge. It appears he had a fine time. He struck up a friendship with one of Mrs. Tyler's younger sisters, Mary Mildred Bristow (known as Mildred).

Shortly afterwards, Mildred sent Archie a rather flirtatious postcard. To properly appreciate what she has to say, one must understand that there was, and is, a well-known dance studio in Hereford, England, known as the Sarah Jane School of Dancing.

HOLY CROSS HOME,
CLENT,
WORCESTERSHIRE.

I was so pleased to see you, and shall like to know how you are when you get to Ramsgate, and to hear that you are safely home to Canada, using your wooden arm to support your partner. Still raining. Good luck from (Sarah Jane) M.M.B.

On August 28, Mrs. Tyler wrote to Elísabet completing a letter that Archie had begun. She does not mention that Archie fell ill while staying at her home. She does mention that she often receives a card from Pete Olson but he has not visited her as yet.

Pete never did take Mrs. Tyler up on her invitation. He was killed in action on August 16, 1918 during the aftermath of the Battle of Amiens. He was one week short of his 34th birthday, and died less than three months prior to the end of the War. Pete left a widow and two young children.

SUNDAY AUG 26 1917
Dear Mother,
I am writing this at Mrs. Tyler's. I have had a splendid time. My leave started.

TUESDAY 28TH
Dear Mrs Polson,
I hope that you are all well. I am, as you will see, finishing the letter that Archie started writing to you on Sunday, and he asked me to write for him as a friend of ours called to take him for a drive. He was with us four days. A wire came for him yesterday to report today at Ramsgate, and I hope that in a few days he will be on his way home to Canada. I pray he may have a safe journey home to you all.

He looked much better for his few days here. Mildred and Dot, two of my sisters, came for a few days to see him. Nellie, the other sister, was meeting him at Paddington station last night so that he will be able to tell my brother [Herbert Bristow, the Polsons' neighbor] about us all. He left here at 4:15 yesterday.

It is a mercy he was not killed in France. His right arm is quite off, but he is very brave, and can do most things for himself. I am sure that he'll soon get quite strong when he is home with you all. It was a pleasure to us to have him, and we should have liked to have kept him longer.

This war is awful and there seems to be no end. We have many wounded about here. Archie will tell you all the news about us all, and I am sure my dear brother will like to hear about us.

We think that Archie is grand, the way he writes so well with his left arm. The weather has been awful here. Rain, day after day. It is very serious for the crops, and things are all so dear. When this awful war is over, we hope, with luck, to come over to visit you all. I often get a card from Pete Olson. He has not been to see us yet.

Lieutenant Tyler came today. He has ten days leave from France. Please give my love to my brother and family, and say that I will write soon. Archie will tell you that I have not much spare time for letters. I have not had a maid for two years, and we get many visitors in the summer. With kind regards to you all, and hoping soon to hear that Archie is safely home.

Yours sincerely,
M.C. Tyler.

CHAPTER EIGHT

WITHOUT A FAREWELL

CIRCUMSTANCES OF DEATH REPORT

UNIT.   2nd Canadian Division Machine Gun Company

NAME.   Archibald John Polson

RANK.   Pte.   NUMBER.   721948

DATE OF DEATH.   1-9-17

CAUSE OF DEATH.   Died Tetanus – P. P. Can. Red Cross Special
                  Hospital, Ramsgate.

DETAILED REPORT OF CIRCUMSTANCES SURROUNDING THE DEATH OF THIS SOLDIER. (IF "DIED OF WOUNDS" PLEASE REPORT HOW WOUNDS WERE RECEIVED)

Transferred from Granville Special Hospital on 9-8-17 where he had been boarded for Canada, and had been granted leave in England. He went on leave 18-8-17. Whilst on leave he took sick, and reported to a Civilian Doctor, who apparently considered the case trivial, as the patient improved with treatment. He returned to this Hospital 28-8-17 at this time suffering from headache, general pain, and rigidity of jaw. Considered he had tetanus and gave intra-tatcal injections of anti-tetanus toxins at once. These injections were repeated daily, several times a day. He had an amputation of the right arm and multiple wounds of the body and leg. His condition steadily grew worse with definite symptoms of tetanus, and he died on the 1-9-17.

(SGD) G.B. Peat, Major & Adjt.

For Officer Commanding

P.P.C.R.C.S. hospital.

Archie Polson died just four days after the last letter from Mrs. Tyler. According to a later letter from Mrs. Tyler, a cable was sent to the Polson family by the War Office. Over the next few weeks, several letters were sent from England, detailing the circumstances of Archie's death and his funeral, including this final letter from the Red Cross Society. The death report mentions that Archie was given intra-tactal injections. The word is properly spelled 'intrathecal' and means pertaining to a structure, process, or substance within a sheath, such as within the spinal canal. Likely Archie was given injections directly into his spine. It appears that G. Bovey had taken over from Constance Scott.

WOUNDED AND MISSING DEPT.
CANADIAN RED CROSS SOCIETY,
14/16 COCKSPUR STREET,
LONDON S.W. 1.
SEPT. 6TH, 1917
IN ANSWERING PLEASE REPEAT NAME, NUMBER,
AND BATTALION OF SOLDIER.

NO. 721.948   NAME *Private J. Polson*   BATT. *2nd M.G. Co.*
HOSPITAL   *Princess Patricia Canadian Hospital, Ramsgate, England.*

Dear Madam,

I regret more than I can say to have to inform you that Private Polson succumbed to his injuries on September 1st. I fear very much that you will not have been prepared for this, as his last report was most reassuring, he had been out & about. The immediate cause of his death was lockjaw which comes on very suddenly otherwise we might have warned you that his condition was not so good.

His gallantry in dying in the service of his country will always be a sweet memory of which death even cannot deprive you in these days of trouble & violence, we must all look forward to our haven of rest above, & be thankful that our dear ones are safe there.

Yours truly,
G. Bovey,
per MSB.

Just eight days after her last cheery letter, Mrs. Tyler wrote again to tell of Archie's unexpected death.

My dear Mrs. Polson,

You will have the sad news by cable from the War Office by this date that your dear boy passed away at 10 P.M., September 1st from tetanus.

I can hardly tell you what a shock it has been to us, and it has made quite a gloom in our small town. The dear boy had left only the Monday before, and had made many friends. He was not at all well when he came, and Dr. Mathews, a dear old friend of ours and a person who knows your country, came and saw the dear boy, and also our doctor saw him.

We feared tetanus, and so did the boy, but the last few days that he was here, he was so much better, that we hoped that he was on the mend, and soon would be home with you all. He had passed the doctors as fit for Canada, and was so looking forward to coming home.

His wounds had all healed, but the doctors told me at the hospital at Ramsgate, it was one of those rare cases of shrapnel being carried in the body for months, and then caused tetanus. His poor body was covered in shrapnel wounds, and I wonder how he ever got well enough to come and see us. He had only been at Princess Patricia Hospital a day before he came to us. He was passed on there from the Chatham House Hospital because of the air raids [or] so they told me.

They did not know much about him, but I can assure you they did everything possible for him. He was only in bed three days. I had the first wire at 1 P.M. on September 1st. My husband motored the twelve miles to catch a fast train at Weston. I got to Ramsgate at 11 P.M., an hour after the dear boy had passed away. I saw him in his coffin, and he looked very nice and peaceful.

He was buried with full military honours on September 3rd, and I left directly after. The matron was a very nice woman, and she said that she would write to you. I gave her your address. The flowers were lovely on his grave. I placed a wreath on his coffin from my husband and myself.

There are many Canadians who are buried in the same place. There are little crosses with the name, etc. on, so that after this awful war, should their people come over, they can see the spot where their dear ones are at rest. It would not have been so sad had your dear one died where he was wounded, but to be taken now after all he has suffered, is so very sad for you all.

I am sending you a photo of the college [St. Lawrence College]. It is now the Princess Patricia Hospital where the dear boy died. Matron will send you a photo of the funeral if it turns out well. Captain Gordon, who I saw at the hospital, thought that he knew you all. He is a nephew of the Reverend Dr. Gordon of Winnipeg.[50]

You could call on him.

My husband is writing you a few lines of sympathy. I hope that when this awful war is over, you and Mr. Polson will come over and see us that I can go with you to see where your dear boy is at rest.

You have the honour and comfort of knowing that he gave his life for King and Country, and God has now seen fit to take him to rest. This is an awful war, and the air raids are dreadful on the east coast that get the most. Ramsgate is about three hundred miles from here. I was indeed thankful to get home again after my sad journey.

Dear Archie's end was sudden at the last. I only wish that I had seen him at the last. With deepest sympathy, and I am sure that God will comfort you in your sorrow. I am yours,

Very Sincerely,
M.C. Tyler.

Mrs. Tyler wrote again to Elísabet just over a week later, and provided more details of Archie's leave, and his funeral. She repeats herself regarding some matters, which may indicate that she was still rattled by the events of the past few weeks. It may also be a precaution in case the first letter was lost in transit.

SEPT. 14TH
My dear Mrs. Polson,
I do hope you are keeping as well as one can expect. Dear Archie's death was such a shock to me, that after I got home from Ramsgate, for a few days I was quite done up.

A full military funeral, as you will see when the photos arrive, is very touching and sad, but a grand end for your dear one. I am sure you will feel it a great comfort to know that he was laid in a decent grave. So many lads die on the battlefield. One never knows the end of their dear ones.

I am sure Archie was a good living boy, and quite prepared for death. Matron sent me three photos of the funeral, and said that she had also sent you some, which I hope will arrive safely. Let me know if you would like any more, and I will write and try to get some. I am sure that it will be a comfort for you to have them, and to have an idea where the dear boy is at rest.

The cemetery is on a hill, a very pretty spot. You will see some of the little crosses on one photo that mark the graves of Canadians who have died for their country. The middle floral wreath on the coffin is the one placed on by our hands from my husband and myself. The others were lovely, and were from the officers, the matron, the nurses and the men all Canadians.

The poor boy said on the last day that he was here, how grateful he was to us, and to my brother who gave him our address. I only wish that I had been sent for in time to speak to him during his last hours, but perhaps it was best that I did not see him till he was at rest, and free from pain. He has been a brave boy, and you may all be proud of him. If only I had known that his end was so near, he should have had his photo taken when he was here.

His right arm was quite off, but it was wonderful how he did so well with his left arm. He was at times very lame, but that he said was only the last month, and that I fear was that awful tetanus coming.

This awful war is dreadful. If only we could have peace once again. I do hope that you and Mr. Polson will come over and see us someday, and I am hoping my dear brother will come. Archie was going to tell him all about us, if only he had been spared to come home to you.

They said at the hospital that all the things that he had would be sent to you. He only had photos, etc., three of himself and two that he gave me, that he had taken just before he left for France—but they are not good of him.

He was very happy with us and said that he was glad that he came over. He went to see some Gimli boys at Folkestone the first three days of his leave, before he came here. He had about £3 in money when he went from here. He *said that he was expecting more to be sent from home. He told me they gave him £10 when he started on his ten-days leave and a return rail pass. His watch was lost when he was wounded in France. He was only at Princess Patricia Hospital a day before he started on leave. He was passed on there from Chatham House Hospital, so they told me that they really knew very little about him.*

Captain Gordon who is a nephew of the Reverend Dr. Gordon of Winnipeg told me that he thought he knew your family as he used to be at Gimli for a time. They were very kind to me at the hospital, and I was glad that I was able to go and see the last of the dear boy.

He called me mother, and said I was like a second mother to him. My brother and all will feel for you all in your sorrow after the loss of his two dear sons last year.[51]

We hope to come and see you all someday.

Kind regards,
Yours sincerely,
M.C. Tyler.

The Matron at the hospital, Edith McCafferty, did write to Elísabet as she told Mrs. Tyler she would. Matron McCafferty mentions that the chaplain had no doubt written, but there is no record of such a letter. She provides a remarkable word picture of Archie's funeral which is as impressive as it is sad. She mentions that Archie was the first patient to die in their hospital, which is not surprising since it was designed to care for patients who were about to be sent home.

PRINCESS PATRICIA CANADIAN
RED CROSS SPECIAL HOSPITAL
RAMSGATE, KENT
SEPTEMBER 4TH, 1917

My dear Mrs. Polson,
Captain Johnston and Mrs. Tyler have no doubt written to you about the circumstances of your dear lad's death, the only one in the hospital, and

particularly sad as he was all ready for the next Canada boat, but the Good
Lord saw fit to take him to a still brighter home.

The funeral ceremony was very impressive. The service in the chapel was
conducted by our chaplain, Captain Johnston. The procession was headed by
a firing party and the band of the 36th Northumberland Fusiliers. Next the
coffin resting on the gun carriage, drawn by six horses, and escorted by six of
our men who carried the floral emblems (sent by Mrs. Tyler, matron, officers
and sisters), and followed by one hundred men of our unit, the officers and the
sisters. We followed him to his last resting place in a beautiful cemetery over-
looking the town and sea.

To you, his loved ones at home, our hearts go out in deep sympathy, but
you have a great consolation: he died the death of a hero, and his reward
"exceeding great."

Yours with sympathy,
Edith McCafferty, Matron

Mildred Bristow, Mrs. Tyler's sister who had visited with Archie in
Somerset, wrote to Elísabet after Archie's death, and, not surprisingly
for the daughter of a clergyman, attempted to explain that his death was
part of God's grand design. We know now that her words of hope fell on
deaf ears.

It is apparent that, right to the end, Archie was cheerful and brave,
and an altogether agreeable person; this despite his suffering over several months and the prospect of future challenges. That, of course, would
have only served to worsen the sense of loss among those who loved him,
especially his mother.

HOLY CROSS HOME,
CLENT,
NORTH STONEBRIDGE, WORCESTERSHIRE.
SUNDAY, SEPT. 9TH

Dear Mrs. Polson,
I am writing to tell you how deeply I sympathize with you and your husband,
and family, in your sad trouble, losing your dear Archie. I am sure that the blow

was hard when you were expecting him home soon, but my dear friend, you can only think, as we all do, that he is spared from much sorrow and sufferings.

I went down to Highbridge to see him when he was on leave, and was three days with him. I went on walks with him, and had many happy chats. He was brave beyond words, and so splendid the way he managed for himself. He was so jolly and full of hope, but I said from the first what I feared, and all so true.

I can feel for you much. I am truly thankful that the poor boy was peacefully laid to rest in a grave, and not at sea, and that all that could be done for him was done. My sister, Mrs. Tyler, and her husband have proved what can be done to cheer the hearts of you all. They were splendid.

We all grew fond of Archie. He was like one of us, and we know what he did to help my poor nephews who were taken out a year ago. We do pray for the time when we shall all meet. It is cruel and hard to think of all our dear boys going. I truthfully tell you that I know more than a hundred, and our own, of course, are most dear.

The sad thing to see is how hardened so many are still, but surely God knows best. Your poor boy was one of the best, and fully prepared, I am sure. We must think of him being with the other saints. Every home seems to have been saddened in some terrible way. Mrs. Tyler will have written to you before now. It has been a bitter blow to her.

I wish that you were all nearer, then we could come and tell you about the brave lad. I hope that God will bless you in your sadness. You do feel that there are thousands of others, so it perhaps makes us feel that we are not the only ones who have the blow.

Archie gave me such a nice badge, which I am so pleased to have. A clergyman friend of mine called to see him, and spent some time talking to us. Archie would have so much to tell us, the poor dear, but when the meeting comes, there will be no more sadness. We, none of us, know our time. Trusting that you are keeping up, and bearing your sadness as well as your dear boy bore his to the bitter end,

My great sympathy,
Yours very sincerely,
Mary Mildred Bristow

The Polsons received many letters of sympathy. One came from the Home Economic Society of which Elísabet was a member.

GIMLI, MAN.
SEPT, 17, 1917
Dear Mr. and Mrs. Polson,
The Home Economic Society wishes to express its sincere and heartfelt sympathy in your recent heavy bereavement, caused by losing your dearly beloved son, Archie.

Too well do we know the unspeakable agony caused by such a loss as yours, and realize how cold all words of comfort sound to a bereaved heart.

We feel the fact that your noble boy died the death of a hero, while fighting for his country and lofty principles, will now and always help you to bear up under your bereavement and sorrow.

With deep sympathy and affection, we are, dear friends, yours most sincerely,

The Home Economic Society
Per: Mrs. E.S. Jónason
Secr.-Treas.

Elísabet also belonged to the Jón Sigurðson Chapter of the International Order of the Daughters of the Empire. Given the nature of the organization, the patriotic tone of their letter (written in Icelandic) is not surprising.

564 VICTOR STREET,
WINNIPEG, OCTOBER 18TH, 1917
Dear Mr. and Mrs. Polson,
I, and the Jón Sigurðson Chapter, would like to express our sincere condolences in relation to the death of your beloved son. I cannot express how deeply his death, and your unspeakable sorrow, affected us.

In light of how much you looked forward to being finally reunited with him, your sorrow must be even greater. Remember that the reunion with your son will take place, only at a later time. Knowing that our sorrow cannot compare to the sorrow of the loved ones, we do experience such great sadness to witness the death of our most accomplished men.

Still, it is a consolation for all of us to remember that these young men sacrificed their lives for what they viewed as a sacred cause: To fight for the freedom of our nation and our country. They did not possess anything greater than their lives. For them, there was no greater sacrifice to offer.

In the hope that God will heal your wound and give you strength,

Yours sincerely,
G. Björnson.

The next letter, now translated from Icelandic, is from an official of the New-York Life Insurance Company. He confirms that Archie was the named insured in a life insurance policy in the amount of $1,000.00. The letter raises some interesting questions. How could Archie have qualified for life insurance as a soldier of war, and how could he have afforded the premium?

A clue to the answer can be found in *Winning the Second Battle* by Desmond Morton and Glen Wright. The authors state that "Toronto's municipal council promised one thousand dollars in life insurance to each citizen who volunteered. The risk would be minimal since the war would be so short."[52] They also point out that many life insurance companies patriotically cancelled their war risk clauses for an added premium of fifty dollars.[53] It would seem reasonable to conclude that the Province of Manitoba, in co-operation with New York Life, underwrote a similar measure for all Manitoba enlistees.

In any event, a thousand dollars would have been a great deal of money for the Polsons, especially when one considers that Ágúst earned $65.00 per month working at Tergesen's Store.

NEW-YORK LIFE INSURANCE COMPANY
DARWIN P. KINGSLEY, PRESIDENT
WINNIPEG BRANCH OFFICE
SEVENTH FLOOR LINDSAY BLDG., COR. NOTRE DAME AND ELLICE AVE.
WINNIPEG, CANADA

A.W. NEWMAN, AGENCY DIRECTOR
M.H. GARWOOD, CASHIER
WINNIPEG SEPT 5, 1917.

A.G. POLSON
GIMLI MANITOBA

Dear friend,

I have vaguely heard that Archibald, your son, is dead. Would you please let me know if this is so, and when. As you know, he has a thousand dollar life insurance policy with New York Life. I have to report it to the company as well to let you know what necessary proof is required in support of the claim. Please send me the telegram if you did get it. My friend, with wholehearted condolence in the sorrow over your loss, I am your sincere acquaintance.

C. Olafson
Columbia Bldg. Winnipeg.

The Polsons were left stunned by Archie's death. They could not fathom how he could die after being declared well enough to return home, and were desperate to learn more about his tragic end. Nina's boarder, Miss Denison, wrote directly to Ramsgate Hospital on her behalf, and received a reply from the commanding officer which she enclosed in a letter dated November 8th.

111 ROSE ST.
WINNIPEG
NOV. 8TH
Dear Mrs. Polson,
I enclose a letter I received from Col. McKenzie about your son. Apparently they did everything they could for Archie as soon as they got him back at the

hospital, but it was too late, as we all know your sorrow, but your boy is at rest now from all the terrible suffering which war has brought home to us all.

Sincerely yours
E.M. Denison

NO. P.R. 119
21ST OCTOBER, 1917.
FROM OFFICER COMMANDING,
P.P.C.R.C.S. HOSPITAL,
RAMSGATE, KENT.

TO MISS E.M. DENISON
111 ROSE STREET
WINNIPEG, MANITOBA

Dear Miss Denison,
In reply to your letter of the 17th inst., enquiring with regard to Private A.J. Polson 721948. This patient was transferred to us from Chatham House Hospital as his wounds were healed and he was awaiting his transfer to Canada, and had been granted leave to visit friends. He was here only overnight and went on leave. While with his friends he was taken ill, and I understand he was seen by one or more doctors there, but they did not recognize the condition, and he remained 'till [sic] the end of his leave, although he was not well while there. On his return here, the condition was recognised [sic], and active treatment instituted, but unfortunately without success. Such cases as this, the late development of tetanus and healed wounds occur occasionally, and unless actively treated from the first they rarely recover as this disease has a high rate of mortality.

Your sincerely,
A.J. McKenzie
Lieut-Colonel, C.A.M.C.
Officer Commanding
P.P.C.R.C.S. Hospital

One must wonder about the Polsons reaction when they received a small form letter signed by the British Secretary of War, The Earl of Derby,[54] advising that the King and Queen shared their sorrow. Such was the reward for Archie's sacrifice.

THE KING COMMANDS ME TO ASSURE YOU
OF THE TRUE SYMPATHY OF HIS MAJESTY
AND THE QUEEN IN YOUR SORROW.

Derby

Secretary of State for War

In due course, the Polsons received Archie's burial report. Neither Elísabet nor Ágúst would ever visit his grave.

BURIAL REPORT

UNIT	2nd Canadian Division Machine Gun Division
REGIMENTAL NUMBER	721948
RANK	Private
NAME	Polson A J
DATE AND NATURE OF CASUALTY	1-9-17 Died of Wounds. Tetanus.
WHERE BURIED	Ramsgate Cemetery, Ramsgate KENT.
NUMBER OF GRAVE	Grave No. 664, Section L.A.
MARKING OF GRAVE	Wooden Cross with all particulars of the deceased inscribed thereon. It has been erected to his memory.
REFERENCE	R.L. 25-P-2112/GR

(N.B.) All communications regarding this report should qote the above number.

Extracted from Burial Records, Canadian Record Office, LONDON.

G r7/w Nov. 23rd, 1917.

Archie's death certificate was not issued for almost two years after his death, another example of the bureaucratic insensitivity that had been shown the Polsons (and no doubt many others) throughout. The certificate was handwritten on a standard form and signed by the temporary

Adjutant General, Major-General E.C. Ashton.[55] Archie is once again described as "the marginally noted soldier". Receiving the death cetificate after such a long delay must have been akin to ripping off a scab that would not heal.

MILITIA AND DEFENCE
IN REPLY, PLEASE QUOTE   NO. 649-P-5661
OTTAWA, JULY 8TH, 1919.

FROM-
THE ADJUTANT-GENERAL
CANADIAN MILITIA.
TO-
A.G. POLSON, ESQ.,
GIMIL, MAN.

721948 Pte. Archibald John Polson,
Canadian Expeditionary Force.

Sir,
I beg to enclose herewith official certificate of death in respect of the marginally noted soldier.

W.W. Stinson
for Director of Records
for a/Adjutant-General.
MBM
Q

CANADIAN EXPEDITIONARY FORCE
DEATH CERTIFICATE

This is to Certify that the records at Militia Headquarters show that on the first day of September 1917 721948 Private Archibald John Polson 2nd Divisional Machine Gun Company died of wounds.

Militia Headquarters	E.C. Ashton
Ottawa, Ont.	Major General
July 7th 1919	Adjutant General

CHAPTER NINE
A WOMAN FORSAKEN

IN MARCH OF 1918, Lieutenant General Sir Arthur Currie, who assumed command of the Canadian Corps after Vimy, wrote to his troops prior to another battle: "To those who fall I say: You will not die but step into immortality. Your mothers will not lament your fate but will be proud to have borne such sons."

My grandmother did not take Archie's death nearly so well. One can imagine her anguish, her sense of loss, her feelings of guilt for having let 'her darling boy' go to war. While the whole family grieved, Elísabet's loss was the greatest, because, not only did she lose her beloved son, she forever lost her faith.

Elísabet had entrusted Archie to the safekeeping of her God and had asked Him to shield her darling boy from harm. In return, Archie was mangled and maimed, and then endured five months of pain before, in the cruelest of ironies, he was taken as he was about to return to his family.

Gimli, which was once been Elísabet's Heaven, was now a dark place, where memories of Archie waited around every corner. In 1919, the family decided to start afresh, and moved back to Winnipeg. Fortunately, Elísabet still owned the farm. She sold it for a tidy sum, and with that money and Archie's life insurance, the family purchased the home of the late Rev. Jón Bjarnason and his wife in their old neighbourhood, the West End.

Rev. Bjarnason, the man who married the Polsons many years before, died in 1914. He and his wife had occupied a huge, three-storey house at 118 Emily Street where they also ran a school for newcomers from Iceland. The students were taught elementary and high school subjects as well as being taught how to adjust to life in a new country. Over the years, the number of newcomers declined, but the Rev. Bjarnason saw a growing need for Icelandic language education for the Canadian-born children of the Icelanders. In 1913, he founded a full-fledged academy, later known as the Jón Bjarnason Academy, to serve both clienteles, and the home school became redundant. A year later, the pastor died, and at some point his widow put the house up for sale.

Due to its size, the Emily Street house was not easy to sell. Nobody—except Elísabet, apparently—knew what to do with a place that big. Elísabet and Ágúst purchased the home at a reasonable price, and the family, including children and Maggie, took occupancy. Elísabet immediately began to take in boarders, and Ágúst found employment as an elevator operator at the Winnipeg outlet of the American-owned hardware company, Marshall-Wells.

The house was located just down the street from the Winnipeg General Hospital. The West End by this time had become the unofficial capital of the Icelandic diaspora, and the Icelanders were becoming more prosperous. The neighbourhood was a generally happy place for its residents. The Icelanders had their "J.B. Academy" where their language was perpetuated, their own restaurants and stores, their two churches—Lutheran and Unitarian—and branches of organizations such as the Icelandic Good Templars and the International Order of the Daughters of the Empire. It was as common to hear Icelandic on the street as it was to hear English.[56]

Elísabet's boarding enterprise went well. She had always enjoyed having a full house, and the challenge of raising her family and looking after her boarders helped to prevent her dwelling on memories of Archie. The Manitoba Medical College was erected in 1922 at 770 Bannatyne Avenue, just around the corner from the Polson home. Lárus Sigurdson was a medical student in the early years, and he referred his classmates in need of lodging to his friends, the Polsons. (One of those young doctors married their daughter, Gústa.)

Two longtime boarders were the now retired Lieutenant Jónasson who served with Archie in the 108th, and a woman we know only as "Mrs.

T.", the sister of the Arctic explorer, Vilhjálmur Stefánsson. Lieutenant Jónasson was referred to as "the Captain", in deference to his rank when the 108th Battalion was first organized.

Over the years, Elísabet's children married and several moved away, but 118 Emily Street remained the centre of the family's universe—and there was always room for the children and their families.

A frequent visitor was Archie's old comrade, Ásmundur Einarson, who the family called Mundi *Frændi* or Cousin Mundi. Suffering as he did from post-traumatic stress disorder, it must have been comforting to spend time with old friends, people who had some understanding of what he had experienced during the war. For their part, Elísabet and Ágúst were grateful to Mundi because of how he had taken Archie under his wing. He also represented a connection to their beloved son.

Mundi enjoyed a drink and, likely because of his PTSD, he too often drank to excess. Elísabet, on the other hand, was very much a tea-totaller and would never allow alcohol in her house. But she held her tongue when Mundi would wander over to the "men only" beverage room at the Leland Hotel,[57] often with Ágúst and the Captain in tow. There they would enjoy too many glasses of draft beer with the large group of Icelanders, many of them also veterans, who regularly gathered at the Leland.

While Mundi never had any children of his own, he loved the Polson children, who loved him in return. Florence Paulson wrote about when Mundi would visit while she was still a girl. Mundi had a farm near Gimli and also ice fished on Lake Winnipeg during the winter. When he had a break, he would come to Winnipeg and stay at the Polsons, usually on a weekend.

On Saturday evenings, Ágúst would often surprise the children with a bag of treats, apples or bananas if they were in season. If not, there would be brown mixed candy. Then, Florence writes, it was:

… off to bed we would go, say our prayers, and just as we were falling asleep, we would hear someone coming in the front door singing:

I'm H-A-P-P-Y,
I'm H-A-P-P-Y,
H-A-P-P,
H-A-P-P,
I'm H-A-P-P-Y.

Of course, we knew who that was, we called him Frændi."

One can almost hear the lanky Icelander coming home, three sheets to the wind, singing in full voice. Mundi was also generous with the children. According to Florence, Elísabet thought him too generous. Mundi would join the family for Sunday dinner. As Florence later wrote that after attending Sunday School, the children would walk:

… home for dinner [after church] and then Frændi *would give us each 25 cents or a dollar bill—that depended on the season. If he had returned from a season of fishing, it was a dollar bill, but a summer spent on the farm, I guess it was 25 cents.*

The small fry held that quarter clenched in their fist [sic] until it was warm, then mother would say she would look after it for us and put it behind the old clock on the top shelf of the side board. What happened to it, I don't know, but I guess the hours ticked it away.

By the mid-1920s, the time had come for Bonnie, Florence and Margrjét to find husbands—and they weren't getting any younger. The War had ensured that there was a shortage of eligible young men, and spinsterhood loomed.

Conveniently, Elísabet's half-sister, Anna, was running a boarding house in Langruth (where Archie had once ice-fished) and living in it were several young bachelors. Anna suggested Elísabet send the girls out for a visit. So they went, and before too long, each of them had married one of the boarders. Bonnie and Margrjét married Björn and Valdimar Bjarnarson, two brothers who ran the local general store. Florence married a lawyer named Björn M. Paulson.

Late in 1927, Snyder decided to move his family to California. They dropped by Emily Street to say goodbye. It was November but, being a rather impractical person, Snyder thought that it would be fine to make the long journey with some of his four children riding in a rumble seat of his Model-T jalopy.[58] Snyder told Elísabet and Ágúst of his plan, and mentioned in passing that his sickly youngest child—only two years of age at the time—was to ride in the back, held in the arms of her eleven-year-old sister.

Elísabet was outraged that children should be exposed to the elements at that time of year. She was particularly adamant about the little one who she insisted stay with her. An argument ensued, but Snyder and his wife ultimately relented, and Elísabet went on to raise the girl as her own.

The girl's name, Florence Archibelle (after her cousins, Florence and Archie), meant that Elísabet now had two daughters with the same first name. The two Florences became known as Florence "A" and Florence "N" respectively.

Elísabet maintained her reputation for hospitality and caring. Florence Paulson wrote about an old Icelander who they called Sloughfoot:

The verandah rocker had many trips, to and fro, and one night it was really on the go. We heard it creak for at least an hour when someone rang the doorbell. It was Sloughfoot asking for a glass of water. Mother asked him in for coffee. It was a long drink of water; he stayed for a couple of months.

Florence remembered Sloughfoot as being rather eccentric.

You would think that a person who has reached the age of three score years and ten would not dislike having grey hair, but Sloughfoot tried to remedy that by soaking red Christmas paper and applying the dye to his hair. Not only did he have a "carrot top," but his forehead broke out in a rash. Mother took him over to the outdoor clinic at the General Hospital. The doctors must have been baffled as they could not diagnose it. It came out that the red paper dye was just too strong for his baby-like complexion.

Over the years, the sad memories of Elísabet's life in Gimli faded somewhat, and she never missed the Icelandic Festival in Gimli—Islendingadagurinn—held annually on the August long weekend.

In 1939, the hospital announced expansion plans, and effectively expropriated the Polsons' Emily Street home. The house had become too much for them anyway, since Elísabet and Ágúst were elderly by now. Maggie was dead, and the children were making lives of their own.

Their daughter Lena was married to Paul Goodman,[59] a professional hockey player who played most notably for the Chicago Black Hawks,[60] and they lived in the United States for much of the year. The Goodmans purchased a home at 652 Goulding Street, about half a block north of Portage Avenue, and it was agreed that Elísabet and Ágúst would live there.

With the move to Winnipeg, the rest of the Polson family had rejoined First Lutheran Church, the spiritual home of the great majority of Winnipeg's Icelanders. They attended church every Sunday, sometimes again in the evening for Icelandic language service, but never Elísabet. While she did not formally reject the church, apparently for the sake of appearances, she absolutely refused to cross its threshold. Instead, Elísabet consulted with a psychic named Mrs. Gíslason whenever she wanted advice, and on occasion tried to contact her Archie "on the other side."

Inez Rinn, Bonnie's daughter, spoke about Elísabet's loss of her faith. "Amma routinely consulted with a clairvoyant named Mrs. Gíslason whenever anything big was happening in the family. She also did some really weird things, like participating in séances. My mom didn't like to talk much about that, because I think that she was embarrassed. Amma had been a staunch churchgoer, but she went completely away from the church after Archie died."

So steadfast was Elísabet in her rejection of Christianity, that when Ágúst passed away in 1944, her children did not know whether she would attend the funeral.

"Everyone was afraid to ask," Lena's daughter, Sue Taylor later recalled. "Then, just as we were leaving for the funeral, Amma put on her coat and joined us."

Sue said she would never forget the day of the funeral. "I remember Amma standing beside the open casket, greeting everyone as they filed by to pay their respects. That is clear in my mind, because it was the only time that I ever saw Amma inside the Church. She always told us [the grandchildren] that sitting in the pew hurt the veins in her legs."

By this time, Paul's hockey career was over. The Goodmans had come home for good, and Paul became a partner in a local electrical contracting firm. After Ágúst's death, Elísabet insisted on moving into a converted sun room on the second floor of their house.

Lena's sister, Fjóla, my mother, had married Paul's younger brother, Arthur, during World War Two. Arthur was in the Air Force at the time, so they postponed having children. After the war, Fjóla lost her first child in childbirth, but I was born in 1949, and my brother Paul, named for our uncle, was born a year and a half later.

Arthur was an electrician, and went to work for Paul when he was discharged from the service. Needless to say, my mother and her sister were close, and the two couples never lived more than a few minutes apart. For a time, our family occupied the second floor of the duplex next door to Lena's house.

Life on Goulding Street was great fun for us boys. Every week, for instance, Joe Dovelman came around with his vegetable wagon. He would let us ride with him to the end of the street. Sometimes, he even let us hold the reins. But the highlight of our young lives was spending time with our grandmother every day.

Elísabet kept Archie's letters stored in a drawer in Ágúst's old roll-top desk. Once in a while, when she felt she could bear to do it, she would take the letters out, and read them again. As time passed, Elísabet's health failed, and the home visits from her doctor, Archie's old friend Lárus Sigurdson, became more frequent. Through it all, she never stopped mourning her darling boy, and she lived in the hope that someday, somehow, she would be reunited with him. On a somber spring afternoon in 1959, Elísabet Polson, age ninety, passed away quietly in her room.

EPILOGUE

IN ABOUT 2008, I learned that there is an online record of every soldier who fought in the First World War. So I searched the name of my uncle, Archibald John Polson, expecting to perhaps come up with details of his regiment and his date of death. To my great surprise, I was directed to the Archie Polson fonds at the archives of the University of Manitoba. I quickly followed the link to the website, and discovered the correspondence that forms the basis for this book.

When I was a boy, my mother told me that her mother, Elísabet, had kept Archie's correspondence, but I had never seen it, and in later years I wondered whatever happened to it. So now I knew where the letters ended up, but I did not know how. Further investigation resulted in my discovery that some unknown person, probably a needy relative, sold the letters to Borealis Press of Winnipeg, who in turn sold them to the University.

As it happened, I had recently retired from the practice of law and in the fall of 2010 was accepted into a third year creative writing course at the University of Winnipeg. As one of my assignments, I wrote about a fictional visit with my grandmother where she revealed my uncle's letters to me. Everything about the story was true—the setting, the people, the sights and the smells—but it never happened. Writing that story planted a seed that eventually resulted in this book.

More recently, I read that The Vimy Foundation has proposed an international commemoration of the Battle of Vimy Ridge in 2017, with events to "include conferences and exhibitions, fireworks, youth-oriented activities and cultural events celebrating Franco-Canadian friendship and Canadian culture."[61]

Fireworks? A celebration? I was stunned, and my grandmother would have been disgusted. She taught me battles like Vimy Ridge are always far more tragic that triumphant. Nobody knew that better than Elísabet. I had an image of her, after her death, scolding her Creator at Heaven's Gate, while a chastened God promised that one day He would use Archie's suffering to inform a future generation of Canadians about the tragedy of war—and to challenge those who glorify war.

I like to think that I was chosen to fulfill that promise, and to tell the tale of the darling boy.

ENDNOTES

1   For an example, see the remarks of Prime Minister Stephen Harper at the
    ceremony commemorating the 90th anniversary of Vimy Ridge.

2   The Rt. Hon. David Lloyd George, o.m., m.p., *War Memoirs of David Lloyd
    George*, Volume 1, Chapter 11.

3   For an example of this assertion, see Veterans Affairs Canada website,
    The Capture of Vimy Ridge, www.veterans.gc.ca/eng/remembrance/history/
    first-world-war/road-to-vimy-ridge/vimy5.

4   For an example of this assertion, see *Vimy Marked Canada's Birth as a Nation,
    G-G says on 95th Anniversary of the Battle, National Post*, April 9, 2012.

5   David C. Inglis (1995), *Vimy Ridge: 1917–1992, A Canadian Myth over Seventy
    Five Years*, Burnaby: Simon Fraser University, 1995, page 1.

6   J.L Granatstein, *The Greatest Victory: Canada's One Hundred Days, 1918*,
    Oxford Press, 2014, page xiii.

7   Sir John Keegan, *The First World War*, Key Porter Books, 1998, page
    326. When Keegan died in 2012, The New York Times wrote that he "was
    considered to be the pre-eminent military historian of his era".

8   Deveryn Ross, *"Birth of the Nation was Terrible,"* Winnipeg Free Press,
    November 9th, 2011.

9   Major John R. Grodzinski, cd, Ph.D., *The Use And Abuse Of Battle, Vimy
    Ridge And The Great War Over The History Of The First World War*, 2009
    Canadian Military Journal, Vol. 10, No. 1, page 85.

10 Jean Martin, *Vimy, April 1917: The Birth of Which Nation?* Canadian Military
    Journal, Vol. 11, No. 2, Spring 2011

11 His Excellency, The Rt. Hon. David Johnston, *Remembrance Day Ceremony
    in Honour of the 95th Anniversary of the Battle of Vimy Ridge*, April 9th, 2012,
    Vimy France.

12 Richard Foot, *Battle of Vimy Ridge*, Historica Canada website,
    http://www.thecanadianencyclopedia.ca/en/article/vimy-ridge/

13 Desmond Morton, OC, CD, FRSC , *Significance of Vimy Ridge*, The Vimy Foundation website, www.vimyfoundation.ca/significance-of-vimy-ridge/

14 Ceris Schrader, *Lady Lost Three Sons*, http://www.hellfire-corner.demon.co.uk/ceris.htm.

15 Thuriður Elísabet went by her second name, but to avoid confusion, the writer refers to her as Thuriður.

16 Gísli's grandfather was a famous writer and folklore collector, Gísli Konráðsson, his uncle, linguist Konráð Gíslason, and his first cousin, Indridi Einarsson, a playwright and economist.

17 Nelson Gerrard, *Icelandic River Saga: A History of the Icelandic River and Ísafold Settlement*, Saga Publications and Research, page 2.

18 *Ibid*, page 32.

19 An undated article from the *Winnipeg Free Press*.

20 Ironically, while the stereotype is generally accurate, some Icelanders have darker colouring. Elísabet's mother, for example, had jet black hair, dark eyes and an olive complexion. Interestingly, Thuriður also had what could be called aboriginal features; that is to say, an aquiline nose and prominent cheekbones. Geneticists have recently published evidence establishing that many Icelanders are descended from a First Nations woman of the now-extinct Beothuk tribe. In the 11th century, Vikings from Iceland established a settlement in L'Anse aux Meadows in Newfoundland. It has been suggested that the Beothuk woman was a captive who the Vikings brought home with them when they abandoned the settlement.

21 It is said that Ágúst's brother, Jóhann, was first to change his name to Polson while working on the railway. His inspiration was likely Polson Avenue in Winnipeg, named after a Selkirk Settler, Hugh Polson. Ágúst and his other brother, Snyder, also changed their surnames for the sake of consistency. Ágúst thereafter went by A.G. Polson for Ágúst Gunnarson Polson.

22 The baby's name was Elí, and he was buried in the Gimli cemetery in a grave he would later share with Ágúst's mother who died in 1907.

23 The farm house was torn down, or fell down, many years later, and the farmland is now a landing strip for the Gimli Airport.

24 Hans Pjetur Tergesen opened his store in 1899. He was a descendant of Danish shipbuilders, `but his family had lived in Iceland for generations. (Iceland was once a colony of Denmark.) Tergesen's store is still in existence and is run by a descendant of H.P.

25 Rose Street is now called Bole Street.

26 Frank was named after a young athlete and lawyer who drowned in 1894 while canoeing in the Red River. The man's father was a prominent local politician.

27 Florence Nightingale Polson was aptly named. She trained as a nurse and served her profession for over 50 years, twenty-five of which were spent with the Victorian Order of Nurses. In 1987, she was honoured for her service to the VON at its 90th anniversary celebration and convention in Ottawa. She died in 1994 at the age of 96.

28 *Lögberg-Heimskringla*, February 14, 1986. Lárus conducted a general practice in Winnipeg for more than fifty years, and served as an Associate Professor of Anatomy at the U. of M. He was beloved by his patients. At his funeral, the minister described a typical day for Lárus: "Early in the morning, he would arise and head out to the university to teach his classes, then go to his office to receive patients. In the evening, when he might have been expected to head home, he made house calls. If the sick could not come to him, he went to them."

29 The town was founded by George W. Langdon and W. Judson Ruth in 1909, hence its unusual name.

30 Library and Archives Canada, *The First World War, Recruitment,* https://www.collectionscanada.gc.ca/firstworldwar/025005-2700-e.html.

31 *Sam Hughes: The Public Career of a Controversial Canadian, 1885-1916,* Ronald Haycock, Wilfrid Laurier University Press, page 153.

32 Earl Grey is principally remembered today as the donor of the Grey Cup, awarded annually to the champion of the Canadian Football League. (The Earl Grey tea blend was named for the 2nd Earl Grey.)

33 The Bristows were the grandparents of Canadian author, W.D. Valgardsorn.

34 Dr. Paul Mulvey, *Life in the Trenches: Soldiers on the Western Front 1914-1918 (lecture),* www.academia.edu/2129873/Life_in_the_Trenches_Soldiers_on_the_Western_Front_1914-1918_lecture_

35 Terry Breverton, *Breverton's First World War Curiosities,* Amberly Publishing, 2014, page 128.

36 Gerald W. L. Nicholson, (1962) *Official History of the Canadian Army in the First World War, Canadian Expeditionary Force 1914-1919,* Ottawa: Queen's Printer and Controller of Stationery, page 251.

37 John Newton Diary, Canadian Letters and Images, Pre-1914 Letter Collection.

38 Wade Davis, *Into the Silence, The Great War, Mallory, and the Conquest of Everest,* Alfred A. Knopf, 2011, page 18.

39 F. W. Courington, R. K. Calverley, *Anesthesia on the Western Front: The Anglo-American experience of World War 1 Anesthesiology,* Cambridge University Press, 2011, page 387.

40 While the tone of Bradbury's letter is pompous and condescending, he was much more than the stuffed shirt that the letter suggests. Bradbury was also a vociferous opponent of the relocation of the local Ojibway First Nation to the Peguis Reserve in Manitoba's barren northern Interlake region, an act of political deceit by the federal government of the day. In 2008, the federal government finally acknowledged its wrongdoing, and in 2011 paid the Peguis Band $125 million in compensation. Bradbury's stand was of particular note because there were few votes to be had—Canada's First Nations people were not enfranchised until 1960. Bradbury also introduced in the House of Commons a bill to control pollution in Canada's navigable waterways. He was appointed to the Senate in December of 1917, probably to keep him quiet, and died in office in 1925.

41 *Manitoba Free Press*, April 10, 1917, page 1.

42 *Manitoba Free Press*, April 10, 1917, page 1.

43 *Manitoba Free Press*, April 12, 1917, page 1.

44 *Manitoba Free Press*, May 14, 1917, page 3.

45 *Manitoba Free Press*, May 14, 1917, page 3.

46 *The Winnipeg Tribune*, November 17, 1969.

47 Ágúst refers imprecisely to the wholesale hardware firm of Merrick-Anderson Company, founded by George A. Merrick and Thomas A. Anderson in 1879. Anderson died in 1919 and the business was then sold to Marshall-Wells Company for whom Ágúst would one day work.

48 Skúli Johnson lectured at Wesley College (now the University of Winnipeg) and became a professor of Classics in 1917. He later served as a professor in the Department of Classics at the University of Manitoba, and was department head from 1939 until his death in 1955. The Skuli Johnson Gold Medal is awarded annually for high standing in Classics courses.

49 Desmond Morton and Glenn Wright, *Winning the Second Battle: Canadian Veterans and the Return to Civilian Life*, University of Toronto Press, 1987, pp. 31-36, 40-43.

50 The Reverend Dr. Gordon was Charles William Gordon, a popular Canadian author who wrote under the pen name, Ralph Connor.

51 Mrs. Tyler is referring to the drowning death of two of her brother's sons while boating on Lake Winnipeg.

52 *Ibid*, page 5.

53 *Ibid*. page 242.

54 The Earl of Derby was a Conservative politician who served as Secretary of State for War from December, 1916 to April, 1919 in David Lloyd George's coalition government. He served again in that capacity from 1922 to 1924.

55 Ashton had a long and illustrious career in the Canadian military. An armoury in Victoria, British Columbia was posthumously named in his honour.

56 While the Icelanders have long since dispersed to other neighbourhoods, the West End has continued to be a jumping off point for various new immigrants—for example, from Portugal, the Philippines and most recently from Africa—but the neighbourhood has never again been dominated by any ethnic group as it once was by the Icelanders.

57 The Leland Hotel was located on William Avenue near Main Street. In the Polsons' time, it was rather high end, but later became a "flop house hotel" and finally the building sat empty. The hotel was eventually purchased by the City of Winnipeg but was destroyed by arson in January 1999.

58 A rumble seat is an outside bench seat where a car's trunk would normally be located.

59 Goodman was a common anglicization of the surname Guðmundsson. In this case, Paul's father lived in Selkirk and was named Páll Guðmundsson. There were two Páll Guðmundssons in Selkirk which was confusing for the local postmaster who asked that one of them change his name.

60 Paul was a career minor league goaltender until he was called up by Chicago during the 1938 Stanley Cup playoffs. He only played in one game but the Black Hawks included his name on the Stanley Cup in appreciation of his efforts. Paul would later serve as Chicago's starting goalie for two years until his career was ended by injury. Paul was later elected as an alderman on Winnipeg City Council.

61 The Vimy Foundation is a charity that celebrates Canada's success at Vimy Ridge. The reference to fireworks and a celebration appeared on their website, but has since been taken down. Annually, the Foundation sponsors the Grande Soirée Vimy in Montreal and the Vimy Reception at the French embassy in Ottawa.

INDEX